Match Fishing with the Experts

Edited by
John Carding

Ernest Benn

First published 1979 by
Ernest Benn Limited
25 New Street Square, London, EC4A 3JA
& Sovereign Way, Tonbridge, Kent, TN9 1RW

ISBN 0 510-22519-5
     0 510-22520-9 Pbk

Contents

For Toppy

Preface

In the short space of this book it proves impossible to pack in all we would like to say and pass on to the reader. Some match fishing techniques haven't been discussed at all, and others just touched upon. But consider the techniques that *are* here. Master them. It will take you many seasons, and by that time you will have developed your own techniques and styles, building upon those described in this book.

All the contributors to this book have been forthcoming in telling you as much as they can in the space provided them, and no one has held back with any information. The true professionals are always anxious to pass on all they know to help further their sport, not only (as you will discover) in the following pages, but on the river bank, in the queue for the draw or after the match.

Of course there are a few anglers who will deliberately give misleading information, but they are what we know as 'shooting stars', here today and gone tomorrow. They probably don't divulge information for the simple reason they don't have any. All they have is an exceptional run at the draw bag and then . . . obscurity.

I would like to acknowledge my debt to Mike Winney for his help and advice; to Jim Lauritz for both choosing and taking many of the photographs; and to David Hall, Rosalind 'Toppy' Notley, and Jill Adam whose combination of tolerance and assistance saw the whole thing through. But most of all I should like to pay tribute to the high skill and versatility of the expert match fishermen whose contributions will be seen as the essential feature of this book, a volume with which I count it a privilege to be associated.

John Carding

England International, Mark Downes, being watched by some of tomorrow's stars (© Jim Lauritz)

Match Fishing Today

The title of this book, *Match Fishing with the Experts*, probably conjures up visions in many readers' minds of instant answers to all the problems that they have ever come up against whilst fishing under match conditions. Sadly, that isn't the case. A four volume encyclopedia of match fishing still wouldn't give all the answers; the reader must be content, therefore, to digest the knowledge in the following pages and then apply his skills to the methods discussed.

It would have been comparatively easy to get a dozen of the biggest names in match angling to write a chapter on a certain topic, put them all together and bring the book out that way. Instead, the particular selection of contributors in the coming chapters has made it possible to throw entirely new light on match fishing today. You won't find page upon page of diagrams telling you what a stickfloat looks like; we assume you know that. What you will find is some of the up and coming, and leading, exponents of various styles talking about their approach in a way that should be easily understood.

There are many gaps in the book, subjects which haven't been touched on, and the styles of the various contributors are as different as the anglers themselves. That is just the way it should be; it allows a lot more to come out.

Angling is taking on a new image. It is frequently cited as Britain's largest participant sport and now the leaning is towards professionalism, in team events, clothing and sponsorship. The days of the welly-booted, cloth-capped angler look as though they are numbered, at least in match fishing, the one branch of the sport that is getting things done in plenty of directions.

Several chapters of this book emphasize the professional approach to contemporary match angling. It is this philosophy on which the future of our sport is going to depend a great deal. So bleak fishing and other small fish tactics may not be important to many match anglers, especially our north country cousins on the east coast or the regulars of the Wye and Severn, but to many anglers they offer the basis of their sport. Conversely, lobbing great swimfeeders thirty yards into the Trent may seem very remote to someone whose idea of a swimfeeder is a small Feederlink and a 1 lb bottom.

The point of it all is that team events are becoming more and more popular and the competent match angler who is going to fish for a team, in a National or a river championship, just has to know how to deal with all eventualities if he is to be worth his place. No longer can he bury his head in the sand and say, 'I don't like the feeder and I'm not fishing it', because if that's the method then he's going to get shown the way home if he tries to learn on the day. Take, for example, the chapter on meat fishing by Ron Lees. Chub abound in most of our match rivers and unless you've gone into the method very carefully, you will probably think that there's no more to it than sticking a cube of meat on the hook and throwing out and putting your rod in the rest. After you've read the chapter, I think you will have your eyes opened. It will be another valuable method that you're going to have at your disposal, and somewhere along the way, in your match fishing career, you may well be faced with a peg that is going to respond to the meat.

In match fishing today sponsorship is the word on every angler's lips. The big tackle firms have taken the initiative and their success has prompted smaller firms to put money back into the sport at all levels. To continue this healthy trend, it is important that match anglers give the sponsors something in return. A team which combines match success with being smartly turned out, and attracts the attention of the media to gain more coverage, especially on television, is one which makes potential sponsors sit up and take notice. The chapter on clothing stresses this point and so I won't labour it here; suffice to say that sponsorship and television coverage is going to elevate the sport from ground level to respectable heights, and not before time.

Apart from seeing the sport gets the accolade it richly deserves, it must also be remembered that tomorrow's stars are today's up and coming juniors, and it is to them that we will be looking in the future. They need every bit of help and encouragement they can get, and if the following chapters help to put just some of them on the right track, then this book will have justified its appearance.

Above all, the match angler must have confidence in his trade. However much he reads and listens to and watches, there is no substitute for experience, either in practice or match conditions. There is a thin dividing line between being confident and over-confident and once that line has been crossed the match angler is going to become disillusioned very quickly. He is going to make excuses for his own shortcomings, always expecting more to happen than ever does. Humility is a word rarely associated with success, but in the changing fortunes of match fishing perhaps it is a quality that many of us would do well to cultivate.

The Contemporary Match Angler

2

Match anglers, in particular those fortunate enough to live in areas of the country where there is a choice of several competitions each weekend, often find it very frustrating to decide the best bait and method for any given match.

Even the most experienced matchmen encounter this dilemma. All the top flight match anglers that I have ever spoken to have expressed a similar sentiment, admitting that on many waters it is difficult to decide with absolute certainty on a workable system when faced with the vast number of baits and methods that have worked in preceding weeks. The first decision that has to be made is what bait will form the basis of the main attack on the water. Casters, maggots, hemp, tares, bread, pinkies, worms, luncheon meat, squatts, bloodworm, jokers, wasp – grub – the list of winning baits grows with every season.

Having decided on your main bait, you then face the second problem: How to present and feed it on the day? Whether to leger, swimfeed, or float fish, and so it goes on, with the pole now adding another dimension.

The permutations of bait and tackle are obviously endless, so how should we approach a match to ensure ourselves the greatest possible chance of success?

The successful matchman will have achieved a proficiency in the use of tackle and baits, in the manner mentioned, and will also have the ability to adapt to any style on the day. One of the commonest mistakes made by competitors is having too rigid an approach. The tendency to enter a match with a preconceived idea of how to tackle the water is a calculated, long-odds gamble. If you have the method from the start, then you are cutting the field down straight away. If not, then you're out of it if you persist for too long. Pre-match preparation is essential, but having adopted a method and then refusing to change through pig-headedness can be disastrous. Logically an angler has to confront his swim before he can make any decision on how to fish it. Some baits are instantaneous, others take a while to work. Instant baits are bread,

At the end of every match . . . the all-important weigh-in (© Jim Lauritz)

luncheon meat, maggots; baits that need a bit of time to work are casters, hemp, tares; but there are no hard and fast rules.

The true test of a top match angler's ability is in studying his record over at least two full seasons, and seeing what happens when he gets a winning chance after a lean spell at the draw bag. The good match angler will still take the rest of the field apart.

The one asset of every top angler, certainly of everyone who has written in this book, is confidence in himself. The realisation that to succeed he must be able to feel he is doing the right thing at the right time in every match he fishes is a formidable advantage which he can pass on to no-one. It is this confidence that wins the country's top matches, time after time.

Many an angler loses interest in the middle of a match if the river isn't responding as he imagines. The man with confidence will persevere against the odds, experiment with tactics and use a bad draw to put things to the test under match conditions. He just doesn't give in.

Success breeds success once you get in the habit of

winning, but the habit needs to be developed first and there are no short cuts.

Newcomers to the open match circuit should try and forget the idea of travelling too far afield, unless they are going to watch. Instead they should be looking for matches that offer the highest proportion of winning pegs and a chance at least to catch a few fish.

Inexperienced matchmen would be ill advised to subscribe to venues where a high winning weight, over 30 lb, is needed, and the other 95 per cent of the field will have little or nothing to show for their efforts. It is far better to fish a match which may only have a weight ceiling of 10 lb, so long as it is followed by a string of close backing weights along the entire match length.

If at first you lack the confidence in all the necessary styles required to compete at a high level, then it pays to pick out venues where your favourite technique can be employed. However, you shouldn't do this to the exclusion of all else, and so let your weaker points slip even further.

These days it is far harder than ever before to be consistent. The average level of ability is so much higher at present. The number of exceptional anglers, I am sure, remains the same, but there are far, far more good anglers than ever who can now win off the right peg. Aim to get into that category and you will have accomplished a great deal.

3 Float Fishing Lakes and Ponds

Ken Collings

Ken Collings, at the age of 31, is probably one of the best known anglers on the fast growing Southern match circuit. The 1978-79 season will in fact be his eighteenth season of match fishing in the South. A simple subtraction reveals that he started competitive fishing at the tender age of 14.

Ken, who is married with two children and lives in Sutton, Surrey, has fished under several banners, including the Grebes, Tonkers and the Team. With the last-named Ken was a member of the team to carry off the coveted Trent Championship in 1971, no mean performance for a Southern side in the early seventies.

Ken now fishes individual matches under the name of Aikens, the London-based tackle company for which he is a tackle consultant. In team events he fishes for the highly rated Dorking squad. His two most memorable match results are winning the Hampshire Avon Championship and the big Glen Insurance Open. His success can best be measured, however, by his considerable earnings on the match circuit. Over the past five years Ken has grossed more than £1000 each term, on a wide variety of waters.

This considerable achievement shows that he is more than proficient in all types of match fishing, but his own personal preference is for still waters where he feels there is more scope.

Float fishing still waters requires the matchman to adopt a different approach, both to his tackle and his bait list, from those he uses on moving waters. Still waters are as many and varied as our rivers, but most of the major still water match fisheries are under 10 ft deep for the greater part of their area and it is this type of water that I want to look at closely.

The lake I shall be discussing has depths ranging from 3 ft to 7 ft. It contains plenty of skimmer bream, roach and a few bonus tench which may range from 1 lb to 3 lb. It is doubtful that you could win a match by pinning your faith on just one species, so be prepared to change tactics – not

Ken Collings with a typical catch from a stillwater fishery, taken on float tackle (© Keith Gallier)

drastically – but just enough to keep in contact with the fish, if one species dries up. It is important to be versatile and so I generally put up a couple of float rods, with a view to fishing:

    (a) on the bottom;
    (b) off the bottom;
    (c) on the drop.

With plan (a) I would expect to contact bream and tench. Any roach and hybrids should fall to a bait fished on the drop. The bait list could be endless, but so as not to get yourself, or the fish, confused I would opt for maggots, casters, bread-punch and, as an insurance policy, sweetcorn. Depending on the size of the bream likely to be encountered, a quick change to worm can often sort out the better fish. However, I feel I can cater for most eventualities using the first four baits I have listed.

On arriving at your peg, don't be in too much of a hurry to set up your tackle, for there are a few tell-tale signs to look for first which may give you an indication of how the match will go. Water colour and temperature are all-important. The colder and clearer the water, the harder the going will be. If it looks as if you could be in for a struggle because the temperature is down and the water is clear, the chances are that the bites will dry up fairly quickly, so you must take advantage of the situation and look for a strong first hour. Clear water takes less feed so if you are under the impression that a strong start will be aided by a heavy feed pattern you would be mistaken. You'd be lucky to get a start, let alone a strong one!

If the water is nicely coloured and you have some weed cover, lilies for example, then the signs are good and you could expect your swim to improve as the match progresses. Not only will your catch rate improve, but the fish will be prepared to come in closer.

However good the signs may appear, the man who can fish fine, using small hooks, is still the angler who will get the best return for his efforts. A soft rod to cushion the strike is a must – a lot of fish are lost on these venues, especially soft-mouthed skimmers.

Using the maggot as the main hookbait, I would start off the match with a No. 20 to 1.1 lb bottom. With a small hook you must accept the fact that you will lose a percentage of your hooked fish. But if I used an 18 I would not expect so many bites, so in the long run I am better off with the 20.

The size of the maggot must also be taken into consideration when selecting the hook size. For example, a single pinkie on a 20 would be unbalanced, but two pinkies would be correct. Another important factor is to have the best available hookbait, which means only one thing – breed your own. You can't beat a good gozzer maggot for this game. If you haven't time to breed your own, however, a well cleaned commercial maggot, softened in dampened bran, is a fair substitute. On still water small fish can be choosy, and they have far more time to inspect your offering than their moving water cousins. Fine lines, small hooks and soft bait are my priorities if I am to extract the maximum from my swim.

To accumulate a winning weight I must have a target weight already fixed in my mind, and to reach that figure, be it 5 lb or 15 lb, I must dominate the swim from the word go. Feeding is the key and the plan is to have bait falling through my swim all the time, not enough to feed the fish off, but enough to have them searching all the time and taking confidently. Ideally, I want the fish to be in a frenzy and during the summer months I feed pretty well all through the match, not necessarily groundbait, but casters and small feeder maggots. Unlike a lot of anglers, I don't get paranoiac about over feeding a swim once it warms up. I work on the principle that once the feed has reached the bottom it is, in fact, 'dead'.

The constant drop of bait through the swim gets the fish off the bottom and it is their reaction to my normal feeding pattern that determines how I am going to present the hookbait. Another factor to take into consideration is the type of fish that is likely to predominate. If it's skimmer bream, then I expect to be catching on the bottom and I will moderate my feed so that they don't come up in the water. If roach are the predominant species, then I'll aim

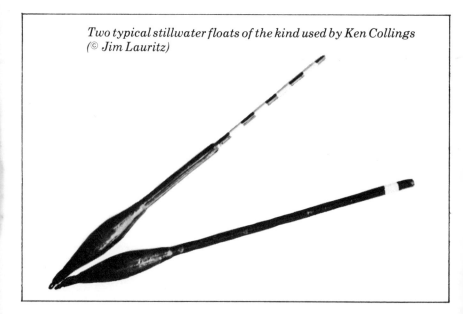

Two typical stillwater floats of the kind used by Ken Collings (© Jim Lauritz)

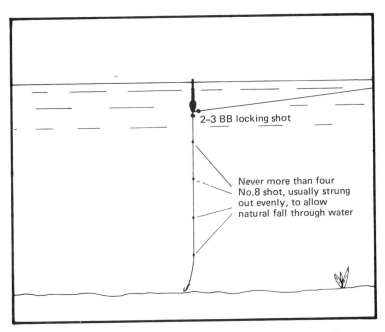

2-3 BB locking shot

Never more than four
No.8 shot, usually strung
out evenly, to allow
natural fall through water

Fig. 3.1 Small-bodied peacock insert float for fishing on the drop.
Float set at depth fish are feeding.

to have the fish on the drop and will feed more regularly to
ensure that I have a constant flow of bait.

I will use two patterns of float for my assault on this
swim. Both are made from balsa bodies with thin pieces of
peacock quill as the stem. I have found this combination of
balsa and peacock to be ideal for this type of fishing. The
balsa body allows me to use a bit of shot which I find gives
me that all-important stability, not only for accurate
casting, but for stability in the water where the slightest
movement, by wind or surface drift, can move the
hookbait and lose me bites. One of the floats has the top
half of the stem constructed from an even thinner piece of
peacock, marked at regular intervals with rings. It is this
float that I use to catch fish on the drop. After I have
plumbed the depth I cast out, without any hookbait, and
count down the bands on the float. Once I have a clear
picture of the rate of the fall, I can fish with confidence,
knowing when I have a lift bite or a bite on the drop, I use
the other float, without an insert, for fishing on the
bottom.

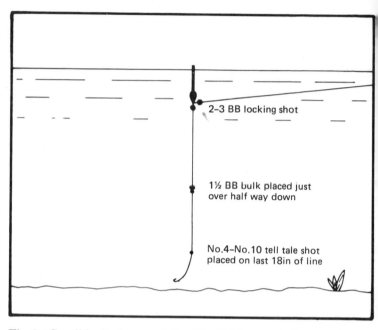

2-3 BB locking shot

1½ BB bulk placed just over half way down

No.4–No.10 tell tale shot placed on last 18in of line

Fig. 3.2 Small-bodied peacock float for fishing on the bottom. It can be set to fish anything up to 18 in overdepth.

For fishing on the drop, I lock the float into place with 2 or 3 BB and set it to drop the entire depth of the swim. It goes without saying, though, that if I find the fish are stubbornly taking the bait at 2 ft depth, then I would obviously set the float at that depth.

The shot I have down the line never totals more than four No. 8s and, as often as not, these will be strung out evenly, to allow a natural fall through the water. The setting of the bottom shot is dependent on the type of bite indication I'm getting, the weaker the bite the nearer the hook I will put that final No. 8.

If, during the course of a match, you find that you are getting more bites on the bottom than on the drop, then you shouldn't hesitate to swap over to the float, without the insert. This can be set slightly overdepth, from anything up to 18 in. How much to fish overdepth depends on several factors, the most important being the strength of the wind and the surface drift. I like to have my hookbait anchored firmly on the bottom; any unnatural movement is likely to be treated with suspicion. The more drift, the more I fish overdepth.

The shotting pattern for the thicker tipped float starts off the same as the other, with about 3 BB as locking shot, 1½ BB just over halfway down and for a tell-tale shot, anything between a No. 4 or No. 10 on the last 18 in. If there is little wind or drift, then use the smaller shot.

On some days you will find that the fish are feeding at a certain level in the water, neither on the drop nor on the bottom. When this happens and you can't move the fish up or down, you will have to determine the exact depth and set your float to fish at that level. The shot can be bunched at just over the feeding level with the tell-tale in the midst of the action.

One of the most important feature in these gravel pit and lake matches is catching the bonus fish, i.e. tench and decent bream. Many anglers have now learnt that these aren't necessarily 'lucky' fish and that there are certain things you can do during the course of the match to increase your chances of catching one. Whilst many anglers may be happy to fish the full five hours on virtually the same method, catching the smaller samples, the thinking match angler will be aware of a given set of circumstances and be prepared to take a gamble for five minutes of the match. For example, if I am catching steadily on the bottom and *suddenly* the swim goes dead and bites stop, then one of three things can have happened. First, I may have overfed them, although this is unlikely since the bites rarely stop dead, they would tail off. The second possibility is that a pike has moved in or, thirdly, a few tench have also found the carpet of bait and have pushed the smaller fish out, which they often do.

Let us assume that the third possibility is what, in fact, happened. I would change to a bigger hookbait, possibly a double caster or a grain of sweetcorn and give it a few minutes. The amount of times that this tactic has resulted in a big bonus of fish has made it a favourite ploy of many matchmen. It may have been possible to catch your bonus tench or bream on a small single maggot or caster, but since time is of the essence, a large hookbait will be picked out more quickly by a large, hungry fish, than one that is no different from plenty of others lying on the bottom. Assuming that the class of field you are fishing against is of a reasonable standard and there is little to choose between many of the competitors and their catch rate, then you must have a little something up your sleeve to give you the edge.

Ask yourself, how many times you have fished a small fish venue and held you own, only to see someone else weigh in the same amount of skimmer and roach but with a thumping big fish to go with them. It is little use consoling yourself with the thought, 'I would have beaten him if he hadn't caught that lucky tench'. It's all very well fishing like a machine for five hours, but it's that bit extra that gives you the edge.

4 Float Fishing Canals

Mark Downes

Twenty-four-year-old Mark Downes from Redditch has, at an early age, established a reputation as one of the country's brightest match fishing hopes for future years.

Educated in Birmingham, Mark left school to qualify as an engineer, since when he has progressed to take up an appointment as a consultant to a leading tackle manufacturer. Mark's match fishing career started at the early age of 13 and, remarkably enough, a year later he competed in the massive 5000 peg BAA Annual and surprised one and all by finishing seventh; three years later he went a few better and finished third.

Mark Downes seen here applying his Midland canal tactics to Kent's Royal Military Canal (© Jim Lauritz)

Obviously the biggest influence on his career has been his association with the successful Starlets AS team, the young match fishing phenomenon from the Midlands, of which he is a regular member. He is also a member of the BAA squad and as such has three National Championship team winners medals to his credit.

Mark has also been reserve for England twice and is currently having his best run on the open circuit. During the 1977-78 season he won eight opens and just clinched the coveted Greenway Top 20 award, a hard fought individual league, battled out against the cream of the Midlands match fishing regulars.

Although happiest when he can offer a bait presented underneath a float on moving waters, Mark also turns his hand to other winning methods and early on in his matchfishing apprenticeship learnt to master canals. As well as being a more than proficient small fish catcher on canals, Mark has also an enviable list of big fish to his credit, with specimen barbel, bream and chub to his name.

Fishing canals

In recent seasons, the general attitude toward canal fishing has changed for the better. No longer are these man-made waterways treated as a last resort in winter or for the 'kids who like gudgeon bashing'. Canal fishing has now become an essential and sophisticated branch of match angling, especially in team events, and the approach requires the ultimate in finesse. Both the quantity and quality of fish to be caught has improved enormously. Before enlarging on the tackle and approach needed for canal fishing, I think it best to describe the general make-up and geography of canals and the fish dispersion in them. This will give us a clearer picture of what we are up against.

The canal

As we know, canals were initially built for the transportation of goods between industrial areas. Over the years the constant boat traffic has changed the profile

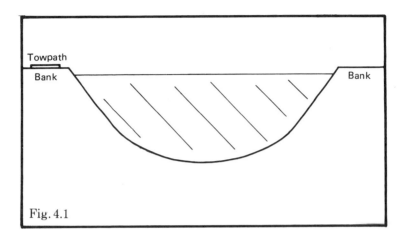

Fig. 4.1

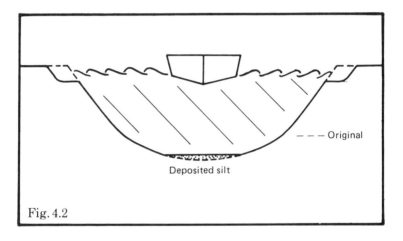

Original

Deposited silt

Fig. 4.2

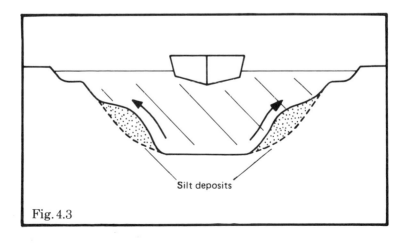

Silt deposits

Fig. 4.3

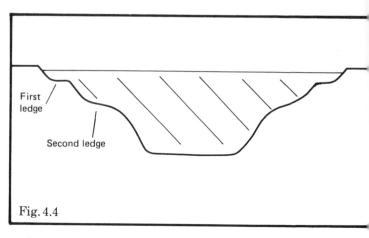

First ledge

Second ledge

Fig. 4.4

of the bed considerably. Originally, the canals were dug to a uniform, parabolic form (Fig. 4.1) with one bank pathed to allow mooring and the pulling of barges. Progressively, however, erosion and silt deposits caused by the movement of boats have created two important features of the canals we know today.

(i) Surface erosion Waves generated by boat traffic have caused the erosion of banks, creating what is known as 'the first ledge' (Fig. 4.2). This is generally no more than 12 in deep.

(ii) Silt deposits and bed erosion Silt and surface erosion debris obviously have to be deposited somewhere in the canal, and because of the nature of the undercurrent scouring caused by boat traffic, the silt slowly builds up on the two sloping flanks (Fig. 4.3).

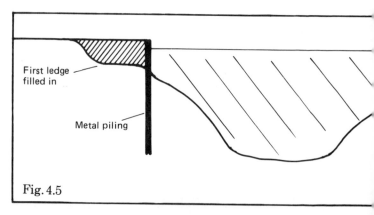

First ledge filled in

Metal piling

Fig. 4.5

So what was originally a cutting of even, parabolic form is now, in most cases, a series of ledges (Fig. 4.4).

Another recent addition to canal characteristics are the reinforced sides, usually in the form of concrete or metal pilings. Their function is to prevent further bank erosion and surface erosion, which removes the first ledge (Fig. 4.5).

Canal movement

Contrary to popular belief, canal waters do move, and generally in one direction only. This greatly depends on the lie of the land. For example, Pound 1 (Fig. 4.6) will flow from left to right when the lock is filled, but will not move from right to left. On the other hand, Pound 3 will flow from right to left when lock 3 is filled, but Pound 2 will flow in both directions as it is fed at both ends, and at some point in Pound 3, there will be an overflow.

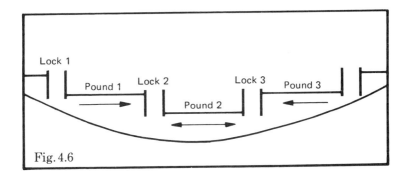

Fig. 4.6

Fish dispersion

Having familiarized ourselves with the make-up of an average canal, and most of the canals in the Midlands fall into this category, we must now determine where to find the fish. Naturally, they will be where there is food and a certain amount of cover and, generally speaking, this is on or between the ledges. The reasons for this are:

(a) any food which finds its way into the canal, from trees, boats, etc., is eventually deposited on the ledges, due to the constant action of the boat traffic.

(b) any food falling off bankside shrubbery is deposited on the upper ledges.

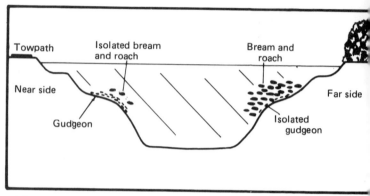

Fig. 4.7 Fish dispersion

This means that the largest quantities of fish are usually to be found on the near and far banks. At least, this is generally the case in summer, but as winter approaches there are fewer boats. This fact, coupled with the fall in temperature and a reduction in the natural food supply causes the fish to drop down to the second ledge where they find slightly warmer and deeper water.

Most of the common species of fish can be found in canals, but generally speaking, gudgeon, roach and bream are the prime targets for the match angler.

Gudgeon   Gudgeon are basically bottom feeders and are often found in very large shoals. It is for this reason that they often make a very worthwhile target for the match angler who is fishing for a win in a low weight contest. When gudgeon is the target we must set our stalls to catch as many as possible as quickly as possible. We would generally concentrate our efforts on the nearside swim, simply for accuracy in feeding and speed.

Bream and roach   The bream and roach shoals usually consist of fish between 6 oz and 10 oz and are generally bottom to mid-water feeders. As the larger fish of the species tend to be shyer than the others, they soon leave the near side swim and are often easier to catch and hold together as a feeding shoal on the far side.

Tactics

It is essential at all times, when canal angling, to be quiet, organized and efficient. Inefficiency leads to wasted time, unnecessary movement and bankside disturbance. For

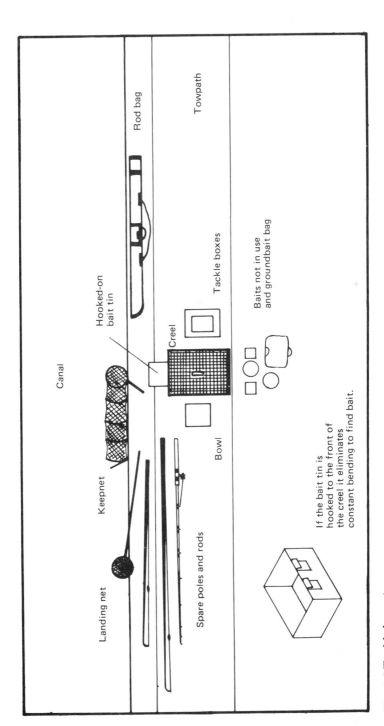

Fig. 4.8 Tackle layout

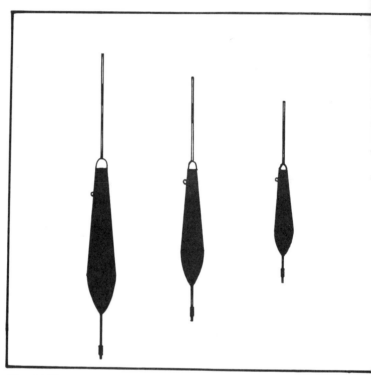

Fig. 4.9 Typical canal pole floats

instance, if one of your set-ups is somewhere out of reach behind you, you will have to leave your peg to fetch it and any fish that may be feeding close in will be disturbed. I make a point of setting up my tackle and then laying it methodically around me, so that everything is in reach (Fig. 4.8).

A useful tip, when swinging in a small fish, is to remember just how likely it is to fall off the hook and onto the bank. In most cases it will find its way back into the water, but by strategically placing your rod bag along the edge of the bank, this can be prevented. Another golden rule is ALWAYS PEG THE KEEPNET AT BOTH ENDS ALONG THE BANK. This prevents the boats washing your net through the shoal of feeding gudgeon.

Now that we have arrived at the canal and laid out our gear, what do we use first? This question of tackle and applications has a two-part answer:

(a) nearside swim and pole rigs;
(b) farside swim and rod and reel.

(a) *Tackling the nearside swim*   Generally speaking, the sort of fish we expect to find on the nearside swim are small - usually gudgeon. In order to obtain a weight of around 3 lb, we need to aim for between 150 and 300 fish, depending on the average size for the water. Whatever size this may be it is the same for everyone, so speed is vital.

In the nearside swim the pole comes into play. These can vary from 3 ft to 10 ft depending on where the fish are lying on the ledge. I normally set up three poles, 4 ft, 7 ft

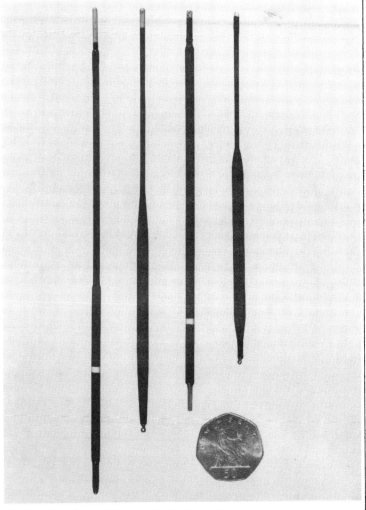

A selection of canal floats (© Jim Lauritz)

and 9 ft, each with similar terminal tackle which will be illustrated later (fig. 4.11). Each of my poles are fitted with the now familiar crook and elastic shock absorbers.

The main line is 1.1 lb with a short 6 in hook length of 8 oz or 12 oz. The floats I use are all a similar shape (Fig. 4.9) and all have nylon or bristle inserts.

The preference is for fine nylon and bristle inserts as these floats can be shotted down, using No. 11, 12 or 13 shot. The hooks themselves vary with the bait used:

Pinkies and squatts – Mustad 275A size 20-22s with the barbs squashed in.

Bloodworm – fine long shanked and barbless size 20-22-24s.

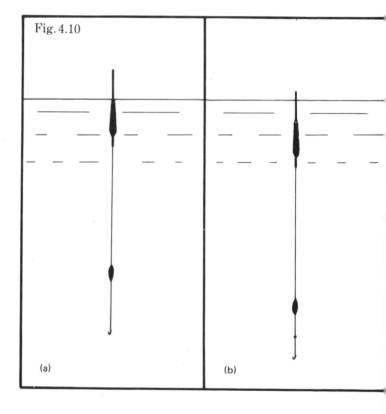

Fig. 4.10

(a)   (b)

Shotting – as gudgeon are bottom feeders and it is imperative that we catch as fast as possible when the fish are feeding, shotting patterns are balanced to get to the bottom quickly. For this reason, our bulk shot is 4 in - 8 in from the hook, depending on how far the fish are coming off the bottom to take the falling hookbait.

The terminal tackle must be shotted accurately prior to use, so as to prevent wasting time on the day of the match. The initial shotting is done as follows:

1. An amount of bulk shot (usually an Olivetti lead) is put onto the main line, in order to sink the float to the top of the balsa body (Fig. 4.10a)

2. A No. 12 or 13 shot is added to the hook length to cause sufficient drop of the bristle tip (Fig. 4.10b)

One point to check on - always shot the float with the hook and hook length on because, in some cases, the weight of the hook is sufficient to alter the trim of the bristle.

The No. 13 shot is used, because even with gudgeon, the bait can be taken before it's fully settled and this will, in fact, give a definite bite registration and the bristle will not fully submerge. By the same token, the lifting of a No. 13 shot will be enough to signal a lift bite on the bristle.

So now you're ready to start trying for gudgeon. As with all types of fishing, the activities of the surrounding anglers affect you directly, especially on canals, where there is little room for error when gudgeon are the target. It is imperative that you consider what your opponents are doing and there are two different sets of tactics.

1. If the anglers either side of you have similar bait, you must draw the fish as quickly as possible, or they may

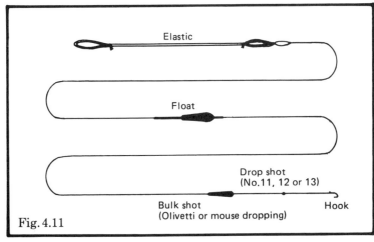

Fig. 4.11

Fig. 4.12 Typical canal waggler made from peacock and/or sarkandas

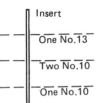

Insert

One No.13

Two No.10

One No.10

Body

Cane
base

travel past your swim and onto the adjacent angler's feed. Initially, you will need to put a substantial amount of feed into your selected swim. This should enable you to draw fish quickly and catch at a fast rate early on. However, your catch rate may fall off with this method, by which time your opponents would tend to increase their catch rate. You will hope that your early fast catch rate will be enough to carry you through, providing you can still add to the lead you may hold at this stage of the match.

2. If the anglers either side of you appear to be tackling the venue differently – for example, they may be using different baits – then it is usually wise to maintain a steady catch rate over a longer period, rather than have a flying start and then fade away. There's no secret to this 'little and often' approach, where a pinch of bait is fed every cast. It will, more often than not, ensure that you have fish in front of you for most of the match.

At the beginning of the match, accurately plumb the depth, using either a very small plummet or by pinching a swan shot gently onto the hook. Once you have established where you are going to fish, and the depth, start applying the feed in *two* areas – one to suit a 2 metre pole and the other for a 3 metre pole. I have found that if the bait is coming in from two close sources, then the fish will move around in a frenzy and so the catch rate can be extended. Also, if gudgeon seem very prolific, these two baited areas can slowly be amalgamated to give one really hot swim.

Once the fish really start feeding, it becomes relatively simple, providing your technique with short poles is good. It is only when the bites become finicky or slow that matches are won or lost, and it is up to the angler to try everything to keep a few fish coming, since it is often these last precious few ounces that decide the winner.

The only answer is to persevere and concentrate, because at this stage every missed bite may mean a lost match and usually only a couple of ounces separates first and second man on these gudgeon sprints.

(b) *Tackling the far side swim*   Canals are generally between 10 and 20 yards wide, and the weight at the float is determined by the width of the canal. For example, if a 2 BB float can be cast easily to the far bank, there is no point in using a 2 AAA. I use the following floats:

1. The Dart   This is simply a loaded balsa/cane antenna which will take between 3 and 5 dust shot to fully cock.

2. Fine Peacock or Sarkandas Waggler   I generally prefer these floats. Basically, they consist of ⅛ in or ³⁄₁₆ in peacock or reed, with a ¹⁄₁₆ in and ³⁄₃₂ in cane, peacock or reed insert. I partially load so the float still needs at least two No. 1 to cock the bulk of the body of the float. A float taking this amount of shot will not dive beneath the surface on impact, something that loaded darts tend to do.

As the fish on the band will be mostly roach and skimmers and are likely to be caught on the drop and then on the bottom, it is essential that we use a slow dropping bait to get the maximum return, so a thin insert to counteract two or three No. 10 shots is used. A No. 13 is imperative. (See Fig. 4.13.) Hooks used are those similar to those on the pole set-up.

Feeding

I normally use very fine brown bread groundbait, laced with pinkies or squatts but I only feed groundbait every five or six fish. Usually, the pattern is to feed half a dozen squatts or pinkies by catapult, every cast. As the tip of the float is fine, drop bite registration is very important and a

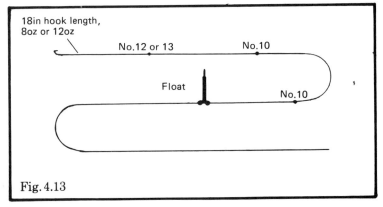

Fig. 4.13

count or rhythm method has to be adopted. For example, if a count of ten is needed to cock the float completely and if, after the count, the insert still hasn't fully cocked, then the chances are that a fish is supporting the last shot off the bottom and this must be met with an immediate reaction from the angler.

Usually, with these small fish, a pause of around 20 seconds is enough after the bait has settled and then a recast is advised. Every fish hooked must be removed from the baited area quickly and without disturbance; any excessive splashing will only unsettle the shoal and what may look like a promising start could well fade out.

If, however, big roach are the quarry and a caster or maggot is the hookbait, the waiting game certainly pays off and just the occasional twitch of the bait along the bottom may often induce a bite.

General

Most canal matches are won by a balanced combination of near and far bank methods. Once gudgeon have dwindled on the near bank swim, it is often the best policy to switch to the far bank to give the gudgeon time to recuperate. Or it may be necessary to change from far to near bank. In both cases, however, it is most important that bait be fed into both swims at all times during the match.

Float Fishing Slow Rivers

Stan Piecha

Stan Piecha is a Leicester journalist, a member of the successful Likely Lads team and a regular in the Leicester AS 'National' squad. A founder member of the now defunct Gobio Gatherers match group, Stan was also for several years captain of the Leicester and District team, before joining Leicester AS.

Since taking up match fishing eight years ago, he has won at least two big opens every year and during the 1976-77 and 1977-78 seasons collected more than £1200 in prize money from the Welland and Nene alone.

His successes on these rivers include two wins in 'Dave Downes' opens, surely events where the largest array of talent is seen on one match length, with the possible exception of a National. As well as these two memorable pick-ups, Stan has also won the Billing Memorial open match on the Welland, another 500 pegger and a 300 peg Peterborough and District Open on the Nene.

Much of Stan's success on these rivers has been on the float, and in the 1977 National on the Welland he weighed in 3 lb 14 oz of skimmer bream, all taken float fishing the far bank, to finish fourth in his section and gain near maximum section points for his team.

In the last three years he has reached the Embassy final twice and his greatest success was winning a Limerick Festival match on the Shannon, weighing in 96 lb of bream – and that was after missing the first hour of the five hour contest.

Float fishing on the 'big money' rivers, such as the Welland and Nene can be very successful, but since the advent of the swingtip and its huge success, matchmen have become blind to the alternatives on those days when the tip has failed to score.

The major contests, some attracting top class fields of over 750 competitors, are usually won with bream and the tactic that the vast majority of competitors pin their faith on is the tip. There is no question that the tip wins and will

Stan Piecha with the 25 lb 6 oz catch of bream which won him the Billing Memorial Open Match on the River Welland (© David Pearson)

continue to do so – it is a deadly weapon in the hands of the Fosters and Jim Todd, who have shown time and again their complete mastery. There have been occasions, however, when I feel experienced anglers have missed out, simply by sticking to this one method and not exploring other lines of attack on the shoals of Fenland bream.

A common complaint after a big match is that competitors have been plagued with line bites throughout the event and yet have been unable to hook a single fish. The angler, in most of these cases, has persevered with the tip, convinced that the fish will get their heads down and he will start catching. If truth be known, on many occasions the fish have been feeding, but haven't been interested in an anchored bait. A good, long-range-float angler would have been able to swing this situation to his advantage and may have been able to give his bank balance a healthy boost!

Since the inception of the swingtip and its initial success, many anglers have been convinced that if they draw on bream, then there is only one method – legering. In the past few years, several of my team members and myself have happily proved them wrong.

Float fishing at anything up to 40 yards requires a whole new approach, but once mastered, it will give you the edge over a large percentage of the field. Looking at it logically, if 90 per cent of the field are on the tip and you are on the float, with conditions suitable for float fishing, then you've cut the field down to size. Ivan Marks is a great advocate of cutting down the odds and long range float fishing for bream is a sure-fire way to do just that.

The method is highly effective and it will give you a comfortable win when alternative tactics fail to make an impression on the day. But it should be made clear that the method has its limitations. By that, I mean that conditions have to be ideal, with either an upstream wind or one from behind you, to ensure perfect bait presentation. If the wind is from any other quarter, tackle at that range becomes difficult to control and thus loses its effectiveness. Having established when the float can be used, the next step is to discuss the approach. Unlike fishing the near bank, where quantity rather than quality is expected, when you go the 'big chuck', the reverse is more likely. The fish we aim to catch are in the 1lb-4lb bracket. As most matches are won on the Welland with 20 lb plus, your target should be around a dozen bream, depending, of course on what size of fish you have in front of you. There are stretches on the Welland which are well known for throwing up large bream and other places where fish in the 1½-2 lb range are more likely.

The initial feeding pattern is the same as that for legering, two or three balls at the start and then keep it going in every ten to fifteen minutes until the fish arrive.

This is where the swingtip scores as you are able to get positive proof of fish moving around the swim by the 'liners' you so often get when bream move in. On the float, however, the first indication you are likely to get is a fish, but once they come play it by ear.

On the Nene and Welland, brown, fine groundbait should be used. In recent years, this has proved time and again to be superior to white. On the Welland, casters should be the main ingredient, while on the Nene, bronze squatts or pinkies should be added. The groundbait should be mixed soft enough to break on impact with the water, dropping in a cloud. Accuracy is of paramount importance – if you don't feel confident enough to throw it, then use a catapult.

Floats

The floats used have to carry enough shot to cast the distance with ease, so it's no good struggling with a light waggler. The two floats which I find most successful

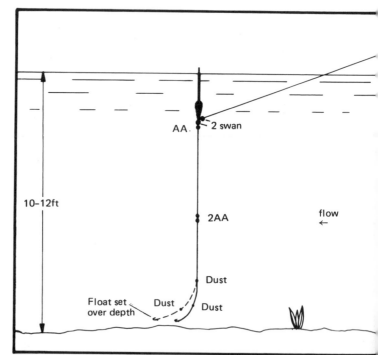

Fig. 5.1 The maxi waggler shotted for fishing a swim 8 ft-12 ft deep

which now have a permanent place in my armoury, are the 'maxi' waggler and the zoomer. The waggler should have a thick cane insert, a peacock stem and a balsa body. Shotting is most important since, done correctly, it will make the job so much easier. Do it incorrectly and more time will be spent in sorting out tangles than actually fishing. These maxi wagglers are all between 10-12 in in length, to help beat surface drift. The waggler should be placed on the line through the bottom eye only and then locked with two swans and an AAA. Two AAA should then be placed on the line below half depth, for example, in 10 ft of water, and bulk shot 4 ft from the hook (Fig. 5.1).

To give the bait a natural fall in that critical last few feet, a couple of dust shot should be spread along the line. If, however, the river is running, one of the AAA shot can be broken down to two BBs. One BB is left with the bulk AAA and the other is pushed further down to give stability in the flow and to get the bait down.

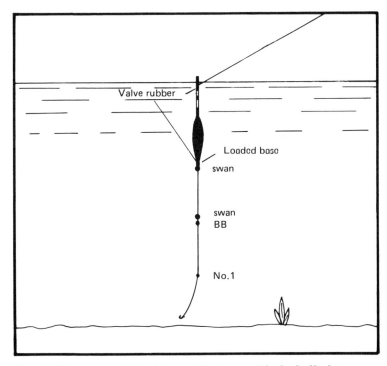

Fig. 5.2 The zoomer, fished top and bottom, with the bulk shot fixed just below half way down the line

The zoomer should be around 8½ in long, have a loaded balsa body, a cane antenna and carry just over two swan. This float is designed to cast perfectly over long distances, to register lift bites clearly and quickly, and to give perfect control at long range. However, because of the nature and structure of the zoomer, conditions must be ideal, that is a slight upstream breeze or the wind behind you.

The zoomer must be fished top and bottom (attached by two pieces of valve rubber) and when casting, the float must be pushed high into the air and allowed to describe a long, dropping arc and be feathered down towards the end of its flight. The shotting is simple – a swan under the float, a swan and a BB just past half way and a No. 1 12 in from the hook (Fig. 5.2)

The waggler is usually set about 12 in overdepth, while the zoomer is adjusted so that the bait just trips the bottom. Because the cane tip in the zoomer lacks buoyancy, and the bulk shot sinks quickly, a lift bite is quickly registered and the float will lift at least an inch out of the water. With a perfect wind, the line to the float can be mended in such a way that the float can be slowed right down and the bait lifted off the bottom and allowed to drop back down. This is repeated all along the swim, if the river is moving.

Both the zoomer and the waggler are cast overhead. Once in full flight, they should be controlled with the index finger checking the line from the spool, until the target area is reached. Perfect casting is achieved when the float lands first followed by the shot in sequence. If it lands in a heap there's every chance of a tangle. Casting, especially with the zoomer, does take some practice, but once mastered, the action comes naturally.

The strength of the reel line is important and should never be less than 2 lb. Remember, there's a lot of weight on the line, weak spots can result if you are constantly moving the locking shot around when altering the depth, and the most likely time for a break is on the strike. Once a fish has been hooked, a soft action rod should take all the strain and 1.7 lb bottoms can be used quite effectively with 18s or 20s.

Now that the essential tackle has been discussed the next question to consider is how far is distance? On the Nene's famous match length, the North Bank, the middle is often the most productive because it is the deepest stretch. At a range of 20 yards, there could well be 10-13 ft of water. Fish at this range along the whole of the North Bank and you won't go far wrong. The shotting I have suggested for the Welland is equally effective on the Nene, but if bleak are a problem, especially on the North Bank in the early summer where they will intercept and crush your caster, then simply move the bulk shot nearer the hook.

When it comes to distance, the Welland presents a different problem. There are swims which have to be fished at the full 40 yards – a few yards short and you fail to catch. By hitting the far bank you win the match. That's how crucial it can be. On other pegs, the middle to two-thirds will produce a winning weight. Knowledge of the river bed and its contours is obviously all-important, but to describe each individual swim would be a mammoth task. So as a general guide, here is a rough breakdown of the Welland's permanent pegs:

Pegs	1 – 50	fish the middle, a slightly lighter float can be used.
	51 – 100	about two-thirds
	101 – 360	the far bank
	361 – 417	just past the middle
	418 – 430	the middle
	431 – 520	middle to far bank

Above 521, the far bank and between 770 and 786, as near the far side as possible.

The reason for the varied sequence is because the Welland is partly man-made to prevent flooding on the low lying fens, but the bed of the old river still runs through the fishery and this is the deepest and most productive part of the Welland.

At the really high pegs, the float can be a real bonus, because of the thick weed which lies on the bottom. Anglers swingtipping can be on a feeding shoal of bream, but unable to catch because the bait is hidden in dense weed. A float-fished bait just off the bottom will bring victory. One word of advice, don't be afraid to fish 2½ lb line direct with a 16 hook, since the bream are big – up to 6 lb – and a lost fish can mean the end of a catching sequence.

If the river has a steady pull on it and the bottom is clear, you can afford to fish well over depth and allow the bait to be dragged steadily along. Otherwise, start just slightly overdepth and ring the changes. However, I wouldn't start experimenting too early. In one Billing Memorial match, more than an hour had passed before I had a bite. The wind was directly behind me and in between groundbaiting I was able to offer loose fed casters well across. As my float made its way down my swim for the umpteenth time, it dragged under very slowly and the result was my first bream, a fish of about 2 lb. The peg, 449, has a history of weights coming from it, so I was pleased that I had persevered. The first fish was taken on two casters on an 18 and in the next hour I added another six bream between 2 and 4 lb. After a slack spell, I changed to a small worm and caster and this resulted in two more fish. Again it went quiet and a switch to double maggot in the dying stages brought two more. Eleven bream, all taken on the float, for a weight of 25 lb 6 oz was enough to win, as well as being one of the best returns on the float in a Welland match that year.

In the same contest, my team mate, Stu Killen, adopted similar tactics on peg 467 and finished second with 17 lb 4 oz. The third man had 11 lb 2 oz, taken on the tip. The day's results spoke for themselves. It was a day when the river cried out for the float and anyone pegged on bream, using the method, would undoubtedly have been in the frame.

It pays to vary your hookbaits. Gozzers, pinkies, casters and worms are all good baits and you will often pick up a couple of fish on one combination then switch to another as bites slow down. Bites on the float can be varied – it's not always just a case of the float sinking away, copybook style. On the zoomer you are looking for lift bites, but on the waggler it is either the sail away, lift or one of those bites which takes the float down a fraction and then holds. These bites should all be struck solidly, because remember, *you have a lot of line to pick up before the hook is driven home.*

Fish taken on the float on the Nene tend to be much smaller, with bream averaging around the 12 oz mark. Hybrids and more roach can also be expected. On the North Bank, a lot more fish are taken on the drop, with the best hook bait being bronze maggot or white gozzers. One snag many anglers experience when fishing the Nene is the number of fish 'bumped' on the strike. This can be prevented by delaying the strike. Skimmers have very soft mouths and should be given time to pick the bait up. The

Nene has not fished well for some years now but in the past, weights of up to 30 lb of these hand-sized fish were caught regularly.

It's not often that you are lucky enough to draw on the bream and also have perfect float fishing conditions, but if you do, and you have mastered the float on these wide, deep waters, your swingtipping rivals may as well go home – they are, at best, fishing for second place. I have confined my thoughts on long range float fishing to the Welland and the Nene, since these are the rivers I know best and the ones which attract the most match anglers, but the method can be used successfully on a variety of waters.

The featureless Relief Channel in Norfolk is one fishery where float fishing at distance is making a comeback, with catches of skimmer bream and quality roach now regularly being taken.

Lakes throughout the country also provide a perfect setting for the method. Anglers will often find that in lakes, the deepest areas are well out from the bank. Only a long cast will reach the feeding fish, and in areas of dense bottom weed the float ensures that the bait is kept clean.

The shotting patterns I have previously described work perfectly on deep, stillwater fisheries, but in shallow lakes where a long cast is needed, the shotting must be kept simple or tangles will occur no matter how good the conditions are for fishing the float. All that's required is a float which will take two swan shot and a BB. The two swan are used to lock the float and the BB is placed 12 in-18 in away from the hook and set so it just rests on the bottom. This-set up works best in lakes with depth of around 4 ft.

Most stretches of the River Ouse, especially the middle reaches, could have been made for float fishing at distance. The middle has always been the most productive stretch of the river and ten years ago the zoomer was a killer in such areas as St Neots, Huntingdon and Offord when the roach and bream were feeding.

Fishing well out with a float is a tactic which, if properly mastered, can be put to good use on a multitude of waters throughout Britain. Try it on a local venue and you could find yourself fishing virgin water.

6 Float Fishing Fast Rivers

Paul Downes

Paul Downes has been fishing for as long as he can remember. Introduced to the sport by his grandfather, himself a good angler in his time, Paul got bitten by the match fishing bug at the age of 11 and the natural result was his joining the Starlets AS. In his first year he was picked for the BAA junior National team on the Oxford Canal, won his section and finished ninth overall. Paul then progressed further, fished for the Starlets on three more occasions and captained them twice.

By the age of 14 he was fishing open matches every weekend and in 1971 endorsed the faith people had in him by becoming the Daily Express Junior Champion on Woburn Abbey Lakes. From then on, there seemed to be no stopping him – at 15 he notched up a fifth place in the BAA Annual, with a creditable 20 lb plus of barbel. At 16 he was selected for the Redditch National team and finished eighth in his section. The following year (1974) he captained Redditch on the Trent National and in 1975 was selected for the highly rated Whitmore Reans squad. Paul has reached the final of the Embassy on one occasion and this season has been picked for the mighty BAA squad.

At the age of 20, many would consider Paul's progress enough for a lifetime of match fishing, but obviously there is more and better to come.

To have any degree of success float fishing in fast waters, the modern match angler must have a wide variety of skills to employ under the many and varied circumstances he will undoubtedly come across. No two swims are the same and as a result, reading the water and deciding on a specific shotting pattern and approach can only be arrived at after remembering past practice and match experience.

Living, as I do, in an area which is rich in waterways, I have had to become familiar with many styles of presenting a bait under sometimes the most difficult of conditions.

Paul Downes (© Jim Lauritz)

Stickfloat - with care

The first type of swim we are going to look at is a typical swim where the fish are close in and perfect presentation is required. The first choice from the floatbox would be the stickfloat and this is the method I should like to discuss.

Tackle requirements:

    Rod   12 ft tip actioned match rod

    Reel Closed face variety

    Line 2.6 or 1.7 lb b.s. depending on size of fish
       likely to be encountered

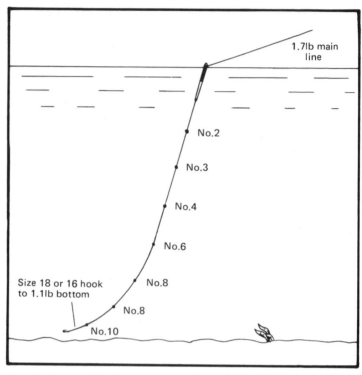

Fig. 6.1 Basic stickfloat rig, shotted 'poker' fashion

Hooks   Mustad 90340 fine wire barbless, 18s to
    16s tied to 1.7 or 1.1 lb
Floats   Selection of sticks from 4 No. 6 to 3 BB

The stickfloat is widely used and the way people slavishly use it under the most unsuitable conditions gives many the impression that it has magical properties. In the right circumstances there is nothing to compete with it. Ideally it is best employed for close-in work, no more than three rod lengths out. Beyond that distance it becomes difficult to control and loses its impact. On the main match water of the Midlands, the Severn, there are many swims where the stickfloat would be the first choice, and if you take a look along the banks of the river and choose and fish a swim, you'll get a fuller picture. The first thing to do is to plumb the depth carefully, not only in front of where you'll be standing, but downstream as well. Any variation in depth could be the clue to a holding spot and you can then plan your feeding pattern and line of fishing with this in mind.

As chub and roach are the main species here, in this case I would pin my faith on casters and hemp, with bronze maggots as a change bait. Having plumbed your swim carefully, if you find a snag or a sudden variation in depth, the opening plan should be to feed the fish away from their cover and into the open. On the Severn, the method is to put in two or three pints of hemp straight away and, drastic though this may sound, on the Severn it works. It has the effect of laying down a solid carpet of feed for the fish to move onto – and they usually do!

Now that the swim has been prepared, the angler must select the right float for the job. For the novice, this can be a difficult decision, but a useful guideline would be a No. 4 for each foot depth of water.

Assuming that this swim is 7 ft deep, then the first shot should be placed 9 in above the hook. A No. 10 is usually sufficient. As we work our way back up the line, the shot sizes are enlarged to produce a 'Poker fashioned' shotting system. (See Fig. 6.1.) The shots are placed at equal intervals to give a slow drop and will also ensure that the stickfloat rides properly.

The float should be kept constantly under check and when it reaches the 'killing area' it should be slowed down as much as possible, so lifting the bait and enticing the fish.

Feeding should be kept constant, with small offerings of hemp and casters introduced at every cast. A tip to remember here is that when a fish is being played, keep on feeding with the left hand, so as not to upset the constant feeding pattern you have established.

If the fish really get their heads down, the shot can be bunched just above the hook length, leaving the No. 10 as a dropper, and this will save you valuable time and eliminate the possibility of catching on the drop, which just won't be necessary if the fish are hard on the bottom.

In windy conditions, commonsense should tell you that the shotting guideline I have suggested is too light and a heavier stick or even a balsa can be used to do the job.

Waggler – the windbeater
After discussing the stickfloat, it seems only natural to deal with the waggler next. The waggler was originally used as a windbeater, and it enables the angler to put his float through at the same speed as the river with the need

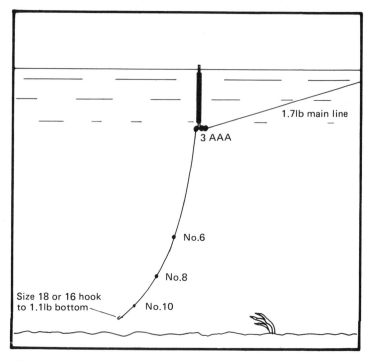

Fig. 6.2 Typical Warwickshire Avon waggler rig

for tight line control. In fact, waggler fishing is an art in itself.

Tackle requirements:
    Rods   12 ft tip actioned match rod
    Reel   Closed-face variety
    Line   2.6 or 1.7 lb, depending on size of waggler
    Hooks   90340 Mustad fine wire barbless, 18s
    and 16s tied to 1.1 and 1.7 lb bottoms
    Floats   Range of wagglers from 2AA to 4 swan,
    thinner, longer inserts for fishing on the drop and
    short thicker inserts for dragging through

During the autumn months, the waggler comes into its own on my local stretch of the Warwickshire Avon. At that time of year, the shoals of chub move up in the water, because the bed of the river becomes fouled with leaves, etc. On the Avon, an overhanging tree or a line of rushes usually signifies a chub holding spot. This will normally be on the far bank. Nearside trees and obstructions do hold fish, of course, but during the match, the fish tend to move across.

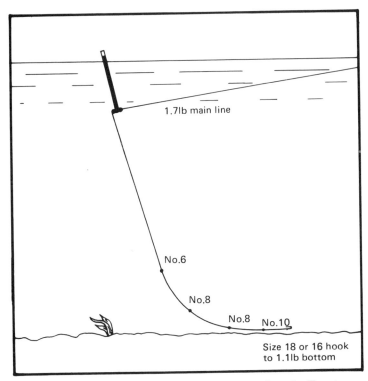

1.7lb main line

No.6

No.8

No.8   No.10

Size 18 or 16 hook
to 1.1lb bottom

Fig. 6.3 Waggler rig for dragging-on, often used on the Trent

Let us assume that the swim can be comfortably reached with a 2 swan waggler and the depth is 6 ft. I would place a No. 10 on the hook length and then a No. 8 with a No. 6 spread over the last 3 ft of line (Fig. 6.2). I would begin to fish at 3 ft since, quite often, this will produce an early response.

By feeding downstream and fishing slightly downstream, the whole swim above and below the feeding area can be utilized. Here again, feeding can be constant and at every cast. Casters are the killing bait, with bronze maggots as a change bait.

As soon as the swim begins to come to life, it is important not to lose any fish, as this may well unsettle the rest. One of the biggest factors in bumping fish off is striking too hard. I know it may look deceptive, but only a very small arc of strike is required to set the hook at distance, especially if you are fishing fairly shallow.

If the swim shows signs of slowing down, in terms of bites, it often helps to rest an area. One obvious change is to drag the bait through on the bottom, using a more buoyant float tip (Fig. 6.3). Depending on the nature of the river-bed, the bait can be fished up to 3 ft overdepth. This has the effect of slowing the bait right down and often produces good sized roach or a better chub.

The river Trent also responds well to the waggler, but it requires a slightly different approach.

Groundbait is often needed to deliver feed to the fish, but on a lot of Trent swims, especially in summer, where the flow is well out, I will opt for two swims. I will loose feed the inside line, about four rod lengths out, with bronze maggots, and I would expect to put in six pints in a five hour match. The other line will be towards the middle and I'll use a wet mix of groundbait, packed with casters to break up on impact. The set-up for the inside swim is the same as I would use on the Avon for dragging through and fishing on the drop. Which to use depends entirely on how the roach react. The far swim must be tackled differently and, because of the distance, we must dispense with some of the finesse and be prepared to fish a lot heavier. I would use two No. 1 as the bulk shot, to give stability to the set-up. These are placed halfway below the float and hook and a No. 6 and a No. 8 are spaced out below the bulk shot, acting as droppers. Ten pints of dry groundbait should be ample, into which would go five pints of casters.

Wye tactics

In any discussion of fast flowing rivers you have to mention the Wye. When the maggot ban is lifted at the end of October, I frequently fish open matches on the river. Given a draw, you need to look for 50 lb of fish. If chub are the main species, then floatfished breadflake is the method.

Tackle requirements:
    Rod   13 ft float rod with straight through action
    Reel   Open-faced automatic match
    Line   3.2 lb
    Hooks   Mustad 202 8s and 6s tied direct to main line
    Floats   Range of large balsa from 4-10 swan.
        The shotting is always bulked, and to prevent
        tangles, file down a barrel lead and lock this with
        BB shot.

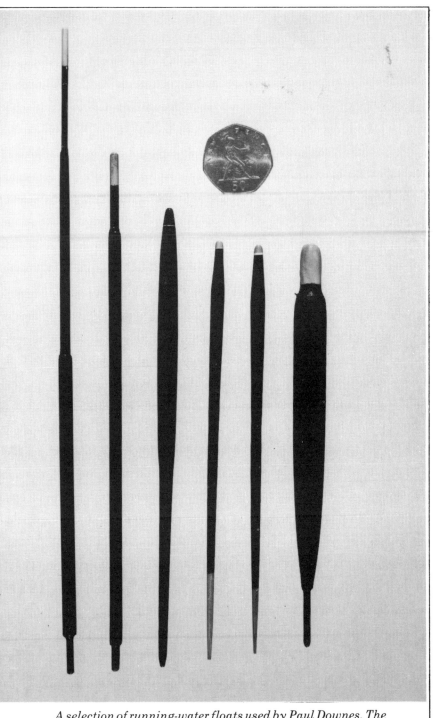

A selection of running-water floats used by Paul Downes. The large Wye balsa on the far right takes an amazing 7 swan shot (© Jim Lauritz)

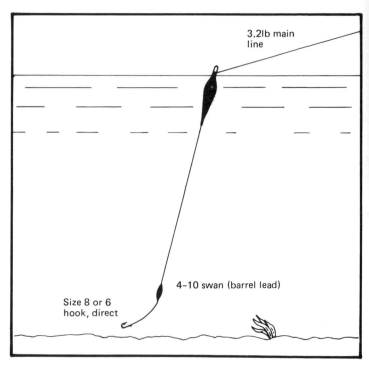

Fig. 6.4 Wye chub rig for float fishing bread

The large shoals of chub on this river are usually located in the main flow and, because of the nature of the bait, and the required distance of cast, a single bulk of shot is placed between 10 in and 14 in from the hook. The Wye is a powerful river, so a heavy mix of white and brown groundbait is introduced to get down to the fish. Casters are added, though they are not a necessity. Hooks are tied direct.

The simplest way to put bread flake on the hook is to break off a piece of the slice about the size of a 5p piece. Press it firmly between thumb and forefinger and simply insert the hook through the middle. As soon as it hits the water, it will swell and cover the hook.

To start the match, run the float through till the hookbait just trips the bottom and strike the bread off at the tail of the swim. This will attract any chub in the vicinity and is an important factor in feeding the swim. When I am satisfied that I have a clear run through, I put in three large balls of groundbait, directly in front of me. Depending on the catch rate, I will continue to do this at regular intervals.

Dace for the Weight

Chub don't always win matches, however. The dace here grow to a good average size, around the ½ lb mark and as they aren't particularly hook shy, tackle can be stepped up to help the catch rate.

Tackle requirements:
>   Rod   12 ft float rod with plenty of rigidity
>   Reel   Closed face
>   Hooks   Viellard Migeon 8408 forged, 16s and 14s
>   to 1.7 and 2.6 lb bottoms. The barbs are squeezed
>   flat to allow easy unhooking and penetration
>   Floats   Range of sticks between 3 BB and 4 AAA

White maggots are the killing bait for these dace. For a five hour Wye match I would take ten pints, plus two gallons of brown and white groundbait. On the turbulent swims I invariably bulk my shot (Fig. 6.5) to give me stability. On a flat glide, a poker fashioned shotting

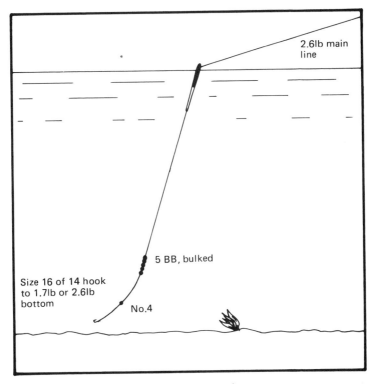

Fig. 6.5 Wye dace set-up for turbulent swim

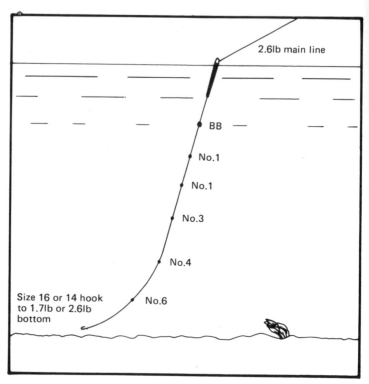

2.6lb main line

BB —

No.1

No.1

No.3

No.4

Size 16 or 14 hook
to 1.7lb or 2.6lb
bottom

No.6

Fig. 6.6 Wye dace set-up for flat glide

pattern is preferred (Fig. 6.6). If the depth is less than 4 ft I
loose feed; deeper than this and you are usually forced to
use groundbait.

To get a realistic catch rate the angler must draw the
fish close in. This is achieved by starting off three rod
lengths out and gradually dropping the feed short until
they are close to the rod end. Landing nets are a waste of
time in this sort of match – fish that can't be lifted can be
brought across the surface to hand.

Of all the types of float fishing I have described, fishing
for dace on the Wye can be the most exhilarating of them
all. It not only involves a degree of skill, but you also need
stamina – and a lot of it!

Legering in Still Water

Ken Collings

I find most styles of match fishing fascinating but, over the years, the one method that has really caught my imagination is swingtipping for stillwater bream. The mere thought of a hungry shoal of slabs settling on my patch of groundbait is enough to get the adrenalin surging through my veins. To be actually at the water-side, watching my swingtip go up and to feel the power of a good bream, will always be a special thrill to me, so writing this chapter is indeed a labour of love.

When I started my match fishing career, legering, in most forms, was regarded as a last resort. As a result I rarely legered, and problems which arose remained unsolved for a number of years. The real breakthrough, for myself and countless others in the south, came in the early seventies, with the arrival of Ivan Marks on some of our big gravel pit opens. As he so aptly said, he 'plundered our southern gold' – to the tune of well over £1000. His wins included a 1st and a 2nd in the two day Halls matches and a win in the Marcos two day event. Such was Ivan's consistency that the luck of the draw could be discounted.

Apart from the pleasure he gave us all, and the enthusiasm he created, he gave us plenty to think about and also, for those who were prepared to watch and listen, a few answers to problems we were no nearer to overcoming. The fact that stuck in all of our minds was the style he used in all the matches he fished – swingtipping.

Before Ivan's raids on the southern match circuit very few southerners knew the score when it came to stillwater legering, so looking back on those times it must have been easy pickings for a man of Ivan's calibre. During this period, I was fishing with a group of anglers known as 'The Team'. We were fairly proficient, or so we thought at the time. It is almost with embarrassment that I now recall how we used to argue whether or not Ivan used a special additive in his groundbait to attract the bream. I must admit it sounds silly, but at that time it was the only way we could explain his amazing run of success. When I asked him about additives, he always denied using them, but also gave 'one of those grins' that still left you

Into a good fish on a swingtip rig (© Jim Lauritz)

unconvinced. Naturally, the reason why Ivan did so well is now painfully obvious and, of course, it had nothing to do with special groundbaits, or any other secrets like that.

Ivan's biggest advantage was simply that he happened to be one of the few anglers doing exactly the right thing at the right time.

In southern gravel pits, particularly those that were match fished and certainly the venues where Ivan was so successful, the bream were to be found in large shoals. Each pit has perhaps two or three of these shoals, as well as smaller pockets of fish. Like other forms of wildlife, these big fish have their own territory and they normally follow a particular route each day, quite often passing through the same place at the same time every day. For the angler who regularly fishes the pit, 'fish lanes' become apparent and the time that a shoal will pass through a certain area can often be predicted. It should be added that fish sometimes can be totally unpredictable, but generally speaking, bream do have regular habits, especially in settled weather, and so a trap can be set for them, which was Ivan Marks' tactic. When, eventually, Ivan taught us what to do, it all seemed so painfully obvious, but at the time he dominated the scene we really couldn't piece the jigsaw together.

The venues that I am going to describe here are big shoal venues. There are pits with large heads of skimmer bream, but these require a different approach. Before the day of a match, it is vital to do your homework and find out what size fish the venue contains. If you are fishing a match on a pit that holds only shoals of big bream, as the majority of the southern pits do, your aim is to ambush these fish as they swim through your peg on their daily patrol.

The trap is set with the aid of cereal groundbait and squatts. Just where to put the groundbait, how much to put in, and when, are the million dollar questions. Solve these and you are more than halfway to success. There are a number of factors which decide your feeding approach. You must survey the water in front of you and - however silly it sounds - imagine yourself as a bream swimming around the pit. Which way would you go? Always look for a feature - an island is a dead give away. There will be food on the ledges around it, and at some stage of the day bream will probably pay it a visit.

It is important to find out the exact contours of the bottom of your swim by careful plumbing - either with a float, or by counting the drop of your lead against the fall of your swingtip. Remember, you are looking for something unusual. It doesn't have to be a deep channel, it could be a shelf of shallower water where the sun can penetrate and promote algae for the bream to feed on, or it may just be a channel that is a foot deeper. If you find anything different at all, that sets your swim apart from those around you; then you could be on to a winner.

If, as is often the case, you cannot find anything special and the depth is constant, all you can do is bait up an area on a different line to those pegged either side of you. In this situation, it goes without saying, let them bait up first, for there's no hurry in these sorts of matches.

Before catapults were allowed, anglers like Ivan Marks, who really could throw groundbait by hand, would outdistance everyone else. Nowadays the catapult has become the great equalizer, and anybody can put a ball of groundbait 40 yards. In fact it seems to be the fashion at the moment to try and outdistance everyone else. This is not always necessary - the fish can often be found on the inside line.

On most southern pits, 15-20 lb of bream is my target weight for a place in the frame. On some days this can be enough to win, on others, you will need over 40 lb. If this seems a lot, bear in mind that the bream on some of these venues average 4-5 lb, so that's only nine or ten fish.

With this in mind, the aim is to have enough bait down on the bottom so that when the bream do move in you can catch the bulk of your target weight without having to feed on top of them, a move which can often be the deciding factor on whether you keep catching or not.

The logical thing in this case would seem to be to lay down 20 lb of feed, enough to hold any large shoal of bream. In practice, it just doesn't work out like that. Too much feed on the bottom and the bream appear to become suspicious and thus easier to spook, or they may pass right over it in a hurry, leaving you with just a string of sizzling line bites. If you put too little down, however, they will either not notice it or it will vanish in a few minutes. After a considerable amount of trial and error, I've found that the quantity of feed that gives me the optimum chance of holding a shoal, without spooking them, is about 5 lb of cereal, laced with 4 pints of squatts.

Five pounds of cereal groundbait may seem a lot, but spread over an area of maybe 5 square yards, it's not much to keep a shoal of 200-300 hungry slabs happy for very long. Because of this, I mix the groundbait up quite heavily. Ideally, I want a mix that will get down to the bottom in one lump, then slowly break up. The bream can nose this sort of groundbait about and actually feed on it, quickly (I hope) getting the taste for more. I put this groundbait out with a catapult, probably taking about 15 minutes to do it. Add to this the time spent plumbing the swim and it's often a good half hour before I settle down to the actual fishing.

The type of swingtip rod I use is made up from a powerful, but soft, blank which enables me to set the hook home at 50 yards, yet is soft enough to absorb the shock of hitting a 5 lb plus fish with light tackle. I use reel line with 2.6 lb breaking strain and I start off with a five feet tail of 1.7 lb line and a size 20 flat forged hook. I don't like too much hook showing, especially as the hook will be lying static on the bottom, so I always try to keep the hook as small as possible. I use a size 20 with a single maggot and an 18 with a double on most occasions. Ever since I

Swingtipping on still water (© Jim Lauritz)

watched some fish in an aquarium suck in and then eject particles of unwanted food, all within a fraction of a second, I've had this picture of bream doing exactly the same to my hookbait. This is partly what makes me use small hooks. If fish are really feeding, naturally, I increase my hook size, but no larger than a 16 which I consider adequate to land any bream I might tempt.

My hookbait is invariably a single gozzer which I cast to the far side of the area I have groundbaited. Patience then becomes the name of the game; you must sit back and wait for the fish to move in. The temptation to keep recasting must be avoided, since, apart from relieving the boredom, all it does is spook any fish in the vicinity.

The first sign of fish is usually a line bite of some kind, not always the great 'sail aways' that you associate with line bites, but also little twitches. This is why I cast to the far side of my baited patch, in order to have a chance of a line bite from any fish swimming through, and thus know when the fish have arrived. To the beginner, a line bite may be very difficult to distinguish from a proper bite. They are normally faster and more staccato, but to be quite sure, wait until the tip has been taken out horizontal and the line is almost taut before striking.

As I've already said, patience is a virtue in this type of fishing; you could wait 3 or 4 hours without so much as a flicker, then the first twitch will make your heart skip a beat. The temptation to strike after such a length of time is enormous, but you must play it cool and wait for a positive bite.

Line bites can last for an hour or more before the bream settle down and start to feed properly. To strike at one of these early bites can be sheer folly: a line dragged across a fish's back at this stage could send the whole shoal scurrying off, leaving you to reflect on what might have been for the rest of the match.

When the real bites come there should be no rush to strike. Once a decent bream has picked up your bait, normally nothing will stop it taking it, even to the extent of dragging your rod in. So wait until your tip goes right up before striking.

You will have the fish for perhaps an hour at most before they move off, so you must make the most of that time. A biteless half hour is a good indication that the fish have moved on. Only after this amount of time without catching should you risk putting more feed in. I generally chance putting in a couple of balls soft enough to break up on the surface, the idea being to try and attract the fish back to my swim if they haven't travelled too far. Also, the softer groundbait is less likely to scare the fish if they are still there.

If you're lucky and start getting bites again, you must

continue with the 'softer' groundbait at regular intervals and hope that you don't scare them. If you can't get the fish feeding again you have to start the whole sequence over again, putting in heavy feed and squatts, etc. The southern pits really are a leger specialist's waters, something that Ivan Marks proved several seasons ago. They can be difficult to fish at the best of times, so be prepared for a few blank days. For my part, I'll always be attracted to these venues, as I cannot imagine a more satisfying sight than a netful of bronze slabs just waiting for the scaleman.

8 Legering in Running Water

Ron Lees

Ron Lees with a net of meat-caught chub from his local River Severn (© Gordon Holland)

Ron Lees from Droitwich is a consistently successful competitor on the hard Severn match circuit. Ron has had a varied life – serving in the Parachute Regiment; working as a professional musician, and subsequently as a foreman at British Leyland. He now devotes all his energies to running his expanding tackle shop business. Ron has been a reserve for the successful BAA squad and has fished two Nationals for Worcester.

Three times he has topped the magical £1000 match winnings mark and has won many big opens. Included in his list of major match results are the Tewkesbury Popular Open, with 35 lb of bream; the Broadwaters Open with 39 lb of barbel; and the March Businessmen's Open. His most memorable victory was winning a match on the Severn below Diglis Weir – memorable because the conditions were appalling, the river rose five feet during the match and every fish he conjured out on the meat was a victory in itself on that day.

Ron's big fish include an 11 lb barbel, three roach over 2 lb and a chub of 4 lb 2 oz.

As well as being an accomplished float angler, Ron has also scored well with bream on the lower Severn. It is for his meat fishing exploits, however, that he is well known, and he has been described as the best 'method' angler in the country. There's few who would dispute his title of 'The Meatmaster'.

Meat fishing – how it came about

This part of my match fishing education came about when I moved to Droitwich from Birmingham. I went down to watch a match being fished on the Severn and it was won with the low figure of 4½ lb, all chub, taken on the meat.

It was a bad day and as I sat and watched the angler who won it, frankly I just knew I could do better and improve on his technique. It was obvious that in winter it would be a winning method, so I resolved to try it. About the only thing that I had seen that I took for granted was the fact that luncheon meat was a bait for catching chub – I decided to put everything else to one side and to start afresh.

In my own experience, the first thing I noticed was that if I simply watched the quivertip for bites I invariably missed a large proportion. By the time the quivertip was moving, so was the fish, for it had felt the resistance and was on its way. But by feeling for the bites and vibrations of fish picking up the bait I got advance warning of a positive bite and my catch ratio improved overnight. It was an important discovery, but there were still plenty of problems to solve. The first match I fished using the meat as my main assault was a Broadwaters event at Winter-dyne. I won it with 19 lb 4 oz and all the fish came from the far bank. It was a flying start – my hunch had paid off.

Tackle for meat fishing

All my tackle is designed with the certain knowledge that to get the optimum return from fishing the meat, touch legering is a necessity.

First the rod. This is my own design and its 8 ft 9 in straight through action makes it fairly powerful. The only 'feature' is the butt ring, which is situated 6 in from the handle. This helps me when touch legering as there's less of a bow in the line and therefore it's more sensitive. The rod itself is very light and is not uncomfortable to hold for long periods at a time.

The quivertip on the end has no intermediate ring, is just 6 in long and is used only for bite registration. Unlike other rods' quivertips, it plays no part in cushioning the strike. It folds over on impact on the strike and as I never use less than 3.2 lb line and No. 8 hooks, I need the rod end to put the hook home – a soft extension to the rod would defeat the whole object.

Reel lines. Under normal conditions I start off on 3.2 lb direct, but if I know that there are some big chub in the area, or snags so that I would need to take control of the situation the second I hooked a fish, then I happily tie 4.4 lb direct.

As for hooks, I started off using Mustad 39082, but they stopped making them so I switched to Mustad 202 and I find these even better. My reels for meat fishing are ABU 506s and I have never found any reason to use anything else.

Perhaps the most important part of my tackle set-up are the flat leads that I use. I quickly found out that the standard oval legers rolled around in the current, giving all sorts of false bites, and as the object of the exercise was to have perfect stability from quivertip to bait, the answer was to use flat leads which wouldn't budge once they had settled. There wasn't anything suitable and, rather than hammer Arlesey bombs flat, I made a mould and turned out my own. These vary from ½ oz to 1 oz and hold the bottom in the fastest of flows.

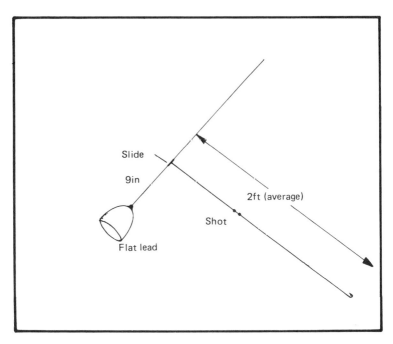

Fig. 8.1 Terminal tackle for meat fishing

Fishing the meat in a match

Perhaps the best way to illustrate meat fishing is to discuss my approach on a normal match on the Severn. The tactics I employ can be pretty well adapted to suit any flowing water where chub are present.

The meat comes into its own as a match bait in winter because, whatever the state of the river, you can usually conjure up a couple of chub or at least get a bite on the meat, however hard the going is. Of course, the meat catches all the year round: in summer it's a method to get a few bonus fish early on; in bad conditions it's a method to catch those same fish, but when weights are down, they could be enough to win on their own.

The first job of the day is to have a good breakfast! I've always advocated that if you are going to stand for five hours then you want something filling inside you. It goes without saying that you'll need plenty of warm clothing, but this mustn't be too restrictive. Your feet also need the best possible insulation. Being warm, well-fed and comfortable means that you can concentrate on the job.

Bait requirements are two tins of meat with some made into paste. There is always some discussion as to which brands of meat to use and the answer is, use whichever you're happiest with. What you are looking for essentially is a brand that isn't too solid and one that smells. I don't cut my meat into cubes, as advocated in nearly every instructional article on fishing luncheon meat – it's unnatural. You can catch fish on cubes of luncheon meat but for that matter you could catch fish on luncheon meat moulded into the shape of jelly babies! All you really have to do is to cut the meat into slices about the thickness of a slice of bread, then simply tear pieces off as you want them. The ragged edges will prove most attractive to the chub and bits will fall off into the flow, helping to build up the swim.

On the Severn I fish the middle to far bank, using flat leads. You'll hold easily enough if you keep the rod well up. I look for bites as soon as my lead anchors. By holding the rod well up with that quivertip in a static position, I can be fairly certain that everything which moves is a bite, so I must respond immediately with a firm, fast strike.

Sometimes the quivertip won't move and the only indication you'll have will be the trembling through your fingers. This is often the stamp of better fish – the smaller ones tend to show on the quiver.

In a grueller you may only get three or four bites and if you aren't keyed up ready, you'll miss them – either that or you'll wait for something better to develop which invariably doesn't happen, and on reeling in you'll find you have an empty hook. The chances are you didn't cast it off, but that the chub have had it. The usual pattern is that you will catch the bulk of your fish early on in the match. Nine times out of ten the swim will die on you and bites will simply cease. At this point you have to make an important decision – whether to persevere with the meat and search around your swim or to go on to the maggot and caster. If the people around you aren't catching as well and you get no response on a small bait, get back on the meat straight away and fish it till the final whistle. Those Severn chub may only be ½-¾ lb average, but on a hard day they will be worth money.

It's very rare to keep the bites coming for the full five hours. If you do they are nearly always small fish. On two occasions that I can remember I weighed in 22 lb and 21 lb and those catches were made up of fish in the 6-10 oz bracket.

If you are fishing with a closed face reel, in particular the 506, strike onto the finger, not the pin. In the early days I snapped off a few times, even on 4 lb line, until I realized it was the impact of the line against the pin inside the reel that was causing the breakages. Many anglers who have tried the meat in matches have mentioned to me that they have held the rod for a couple of hours and not had a bite, yet as soon as they placed the rod in the rest they got a take immediately. Well, there's a valuable clue there. When the angler drops his rod and puts it in the rest, he lets about a foot of slack line off and this releases the hold on the meat so it rolls downstream maybe 9 in. Any chub in the area picks up on this movement straight away and grabs the meat. This is the reason why I often nudge the lead across the bottom and lower my rod tip fractionally from time to time. It brings the bait alive and induces the fish to take.

There are some other things you can do if bites are scarce. Lengthening the hook tail will often bring a response on the drop and I've fished with as much as 6 ft between lead and bait. However, it needs a big strike to make contact. If there's weed coming down the river and it's collecting on the line, where the bomb length is tied, it pays to place a No. 8 shot a couple of feet above the link. This shot has the effect of stopping the weed sliding down the line and when you reel it in, it will come off easily. If you don't do this you can imagine the effect on the fish, picking up the bait and seeing a clump of weed suspended in mid-water, just above the bait. It must create suspicion and it is a problem that can easily be overcome with small shot. You have to work for your fish with this meat method. I recast every four or five minutes without striking the bait off. The only stage of the match I do that is in the first half dozen casts. After that you will feed the fish off and they will drop downstream as the match progresses, either because they have had enough, or because the particles are being swept downstream.

Target weight: Sept/Oct 20 lb plus – up to 15 lbs on the meat, the balance on the float.
Nov/March in bad conditions 3–4 lb (all on the meat).

Bream fishing moving waters - Lower Severn

As most of my match fishing is confined to the Severn, it's not unnatural that I have given the bream on the lower Severn a lot of thought. They can't be ignored, they win matches and there is an approach to them that works. The same approach can be adapted to other bream venues, where there's a steady pull on the river and, preferably, where there's a bit of depth, over 12 ft. The Yorkshire Ouse, the Warwickshire Avon and even the Trent would all respond to the methods I am about to describe. For bream fishing, the right mental approach is a big advantage and patience is more than a virtue - it's a necessity if you're going to be single minded and set your stall out for five hours. Now, tackle for bream. Once again, I use a rod that I have designed myself. It's 10 ft 6 in with a spliced-in quivertip. For reels, I prefer Mitchells loaded with 2.6 lb Bayer. When fishing the bread, I tie a 4 ft hook length of 1.7 lb to a No. 12 Mustad 31375. When fishing the gozzer I tie a 6 ft tail of 1.1 lb to an 18 or 20 Mustad 31375.

Bait requirements are 10-12 lb dry white or brown pure bread crumb. I wouldn't expect to use it all but if the river is pulling and it's a deep swim, up to 20 ft, then I'll make the balls bigger and harder. For feeders I take three pints of casters and four pints of squatts. I've found on the lower Severn that worms just don't go, so my main hook bait will be bread and home-bred gozzers.

If I don't know the peg, the first thing to find out before starting the match is the location of the deepest channel. I cast out my bomb and ease the lead slowly back until I feel the near ledge. I then confirm this by casting out several times and counting the bomb down to the bottom. Not until I have a clear picture of the swim and its geography will I put in my initial four balls of groundbait. Into these I pack squatts and crushed casters - the latter only go in that initial four balls. The reason for this is that once the ball of groundbait settles and begins to break up, the casters come up from the bottom, giving off an attractive aroma as well as being dispersed around the swim at different depths. I believe it incites the bream to investigate and starts them moving around and feeding. Having your tackle laid out comfortably is a great help too. I like to have my rod tip just off the surface of the water and I use a very thin bankstick as a marker board. If the flow is left to right, I'll have my rod at 10 o'clock.

The next job is to cast out across the baited swim to try and get some indication of where the fish are moving. If I get liners, I retrieve and recast a bit shorter and slightly downstream. I've always found that by taking fish from the end of the shoal it increases my chances of holding them long enough to catch sufficient to get into the frame.

After the first 20-30 minutes there should be some signs of activity. With the first indication that bream are there, the natural instinct is to put some more bait in to hold them, but this can be fatal. I need to take at least two fish and then I'm fairly certain that they are settling down to feed. If I've started off on gozzer and caught my first couple of fish on them, and then things go quiet, I'll change to bread. The chances are that this will bring me another fish, in which case I'll feed just two small balls more and switch back to gozzer.

Bream fishing on the Severn, as on most waters, depends on ringing the changes. It rarely pays to pin your whole strategy on one bait for the full five hours but often just the slightest variation will bring a fish. The sort of bites I look for are the small pulls that bring the tip round, maybe an inch, and keep it there. This kind of bite shows that the fish are settled and not nervous. I ignore the little taps as these are invariably liners or small fish. When I get a bite I don't strike as such. I simply lift the rod high and tighten up until I feel the fish and I keep that rod up till the fish moves off the bottom in its own time. It has nowhere to go and I don't want it bolting off through the swim, taking the shoal with it. If I don't bully it, it will come up, and even on 1.1 lb bottoms the bream soon tire and can be led gently in.

The head of bream in the River Severn is greatly underestimated, mainly because they don't show in large quantities, but also because anglers make too many mistakes, overfeeding bring the main reason for people losing shoals.

The ideal sort of day for bream fishing is overcast, warm, with a ripple on the surface. In fact the stronger the wind the better. When the river is like a millpond it pays to feed light and under these conditions the ideal time to get your bait in is when a boat passes.

Target weight in summer: 30 lb.

9 Tidal Rivers

John Smiles

John Smiles has never received the publicity or acclaim he deserves, and that mainly for reasons of geography.

Educated at the Constantine College and living in Middlesbrough, 34 year old John is a piping designer and, being single, devotes most of his energies to match fishing. He started at the age of eight and he says at that time no one would even show you a shotting diagram, let along divulge any information. So he set out to teach himself by trial and error, and over the years has evolved many successful methods for the changing river Tees. As well as on his home water, John's success spreads further afield. Consider his track record and few will deny that here, languishing in the North East, is an angler of immense ability – River Tyne match record, 46 lb 12 oz; River Eden match record, 64 lb 12 oz; River Tees (Croft section) match record, 35 lb 1 oz; Scottish Open match record (Forth Clyde Canal), 26 lb 12 oz; last four National section placings, 1st – 2nd – 4th – 4th; placings and wins in major matches on other venues (Severn, Trent, Witham, Relief Channel, Welland, Nene, Wye).

John now fishes the National for the successful Bradford City squad and before that performed for North Yorkshire and South Durham. Whilst being brought up on fast moving Northern rivers and being a natural float angler, John's preference for match fishing is the big events on the Welland and Relief channel, swingtipping for bream. His ambitions are to win either the National or the Embassy. I can imagine that only by doing one of those two things will John ever gain the recognition he so richly deserves.

Understanding tidal waters

Tidal match rivers are those sections of water, near the mouths of rivers, where the influence of the incoming tide is sufficient to stop the flow of the river and in some cases push the river back upstream. In others, the level will simply rise, but they still continue to flow. Depending on the strength of the tide, it can also make a river stand still,

John Smiles (© Colin Mitchell)

lift and then slowly run off. There are many permutations of effects the tide can have on the lower reaches of a river and if the match angler is to come to terms with the changing river, he must understand exactly what is going on below the surface. This applies not only to the water itself, but also to how the fish react to their environment changing radically every twelve hours.

There are many good tidal match waters, the Ribble at Preston, the Tees at Yarm, the Trent at Collingham and the lower Broads' rivers, the Thames, Wye, Lower Severn, Tyne, to name but a few. They all have their own separate problems to overcome, but they all contain a large head of fish. The major problem is to keep the fish in your swim, once they pass through. Tidal fish are very nomadic and at low tide with the river running normally, they are liable to be packed tightly, often in the deeper reaches, usually in the navigation channels. When the incoming tide starts to slow the river down and lift it, then the fish really start to move around, and that is the time to set your stall out to hold them for long enough to put a weight on the scales. As the pace of river slows down and the banks fill up, that is when the fish start to move around and come on the feed. They will often come close in, knowing from past experience that discarded groundbait and feed has been left at the water's edge, and this is the key to success.

Tackle

The Tyne and Tees are my two local tidal match waters, both of them full of fish. The Tyne has a large head of big dace and roach and the Tees, as well as these two species, also contains big chub. To cover all eventualities on my home water, the Tees at Yarm, which is typical of many tidal stretches, I will need several rigs set up so that I can switch as the changing river conditions dictate.

In a match on the tidal Tees for example, I will have to be thinking in terms of putting at least 20 lb on the scales and maybe more if the conditions are right. The catch will be made up mostly of dace and these run at about three to the pound and often bigger, so I must be looking for about 50 fish and any bonus chub will help boost the weight. As the fish aren't particularly hook or line shy and most of my

The tidal reaches of the river Tees at Yarm, a venue at which John Smiles has had more than a small degree of success (© Colin Mitchell)

catch will be taken in a golden spell of about an hour, I have to think in terms of speed or at least a steady flow of fish once they settle. I also have to consider how best to put something in the net during the blank spells before and after the tidal conditions have been right.

The bonus fish are the chub; they can turn up anywhere, and whereas they can be caught on float tackle intended for the dace, they can also be singled out with a large bait.

To cover all eventualities, I will need four rods set up. The bait list isn't a long one, but I will need quantity as opposed to variety. Feed can soon get lost in the heavy flow of a tidal river, the undertow and then the run off dispersing even large amounts.

My tackle and bait list would be as follows:

(a) 13 ft tip action float rod; balsa bodied peacock waggler; 2½ swan; 2.6 lb reel line; 1.7 lb bottom; 18 or 16 forged hooks.

(b) 13 ft tip action float rod; 5 No. 4 stick and up to 5BB 'pacemaker'; 2.6 lb reel line; 1.7 lb bottom (and could change to 2.6 lb direct); 14-18 forged hooks.

(c) 10 ft quivertip rod; 2.6 lb reel line; 1.7 lb bottom; 16 – 20 hooks, depending on conditions.

(d) 11 ft straight through action feeder rod; 4 lb reel line direct to a No. 6; large open-ended feeder.

Bait list: 4 pints bronze maggots, 3 pints casters, 1 large sliced white loaf, 7 lb groundbait (white/brown mix).

Tidal River Match Tactics

If you are intending to fish a match on a tidal river, there are some facts that you will need to know before the match starts if you don't want to be caught out. The first and most obvious is, 'When is the tide going to change?'. This can be found out from a variety of sources, but the most comprehensive source is the local tide table book. Not only does this give the time of high water at the river mouth, but also the height of the tide. If, for instance, high water is at midday at the river mouth, you must allow at least another half hour and maybe more, for the tide's influence to reach right up the river and so you would be thinking in terms of the river reaching its full height at around one o'clock, the tide's effect beginning around 10.30 am and the water finally running off by 4 o'clock.

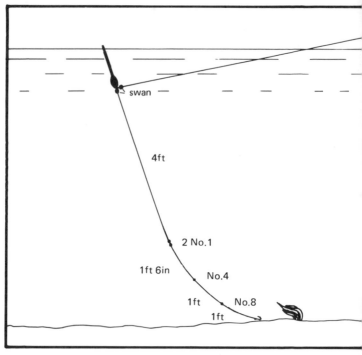

Fig. 9.1 Waggler rig – low tide, normal flow

The first thing to do, once the match starts, is to find out if you have any fish in front of you. On the tidal Tees at Yarm, there are two alternatives to start with. The first is to find out if you have any dace in the swim. To do this, the most surefire way of getting a bite is on the quivertip, nailing a combination of maggot or caster hard on the bottom, right from the whistle. Bites can be immediate and if this is the case, then I would start to feed the same line with a soft mix of casters and groundbait and switch to the waggler (see Fig. 9.1).

The alternative, if the dace and roach aren't there, is to go out after the chub on the feeder, baiting with bread. This again is usually a method which receives an immediate response and if fifteen minutes have been spent on each without a bite, then I have to think in terms of the tide bringing the fish into my swim or at least inciting them to feed if they are there.

The plan is to lay a carpet of bait on the bottom for when the shoals start moving around. If the tide was expected to affect the river after the second hour, then I would

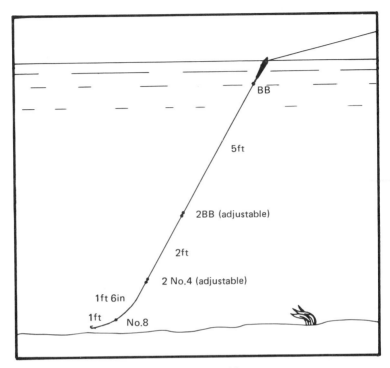

Fig. 9.2 'Pacemaker' rig – up and down tide

continue to quivertip, searching across the river and downstream, still hoping to contact a shoal of fish and still feeding that line about one third of the way across, and gradually dropping shorter to lay a trail so that any fish moving past will pick up on the line of feed and move in, letting me catch near my rod end when conditions become right.

The first sign of the river changing will be the level rising, and it pays to leave a marker stick near the bank. As soon as I see the river is coming up, I will usually pick up all the spare bits of tackle lying around, move them above the high water mark and take up a position higher up the bank.

Things happen fast once the tide starts to slow the river down, and it doesn't pay to wait around at the low tide level. When I have established my second base up the bank and the river is slowing down and deepening by the minute, that is the time to get some bait in. If the river is still flowing downstream, I throw my feed a couple of rod lengths upstream, to settle in front of me, and at the same time I begin to cast short with my quivertip rig, still looking for bites to tell me that the fish have moved in.

As the lift can be as much as 6 ft, then it will be appreciated that the whole character of the river can change. Swims that are only a couple of feet deep and boiling at low water can soon be transformed into even glides; swims with fallen trees usually make good holding spots once the tide changes and the flow increases, especially on the down tide when the flow can be heavy and the fish pack in tightly behind any obstructions. Swims that are a dead loss at low water, can suddenly become 'flyers'; that's the beauty about fishing tidal waters, you get two or three swims to fish if the top of the tide is in the middle of the match!

The match can be half gone and still no sign of a fish, but as long as the river is changing by the minute, then I'm still confident that if the fish arrive, then I'll have my chance to build a weight. As soon as I get that first bite on the quivertip, which can be anything from a minute to half an hour of the river changing then under most circumstances it has to be time to change to the float, and close in.

Putting down my quivertip rod, I'll pick up my 'pacemaker' rig (see Fig. 9.2), plumb the depth, and will use at least a couple of BB well down to give me stability. For remember, even if the surface water appears to be flowing downstream, the lower level may be going a lot slower.

I'll commence operations on that patch of groundbait close in. As the river slows and lifts, then I can expect the bites to be confident and regular. As soon as that shoal arrives, I'm looking for a bite the moment the last shot has cocked, not forgetting that as the river continues to rise, then so must I adjust for depth. If it's a high tide, then the river may well come to a standstill and flow upstream, and I must take care with my feeding to ensure that I don't lose them at this stage.

As the tide reaches its peak, the forces of the river and the tide will be equalized and again the river will stop and then start to flow out again, usually quite strongly.

If I can now keep the fish in front of me in what is going to be a heavy flow, then I have a good chance of reaching my target weight of 20 lb, and because I could be fishing in anything up to 14 ft of water, I must use a heavy mix of groundbait, to keep the fish occupied hard on the bottom.

If I find that I can't present the bait correctly on the float, then I'll switch back to the quiver, to keep in touch with the shoal, and wait till the river runs down a bit and the flow settles. You can still catch at a good rate on the quiver, it just means having quick reflexes and holding the rod in one hand, with the top joint laid on the rod rest.

If, however, the fish are really coming well to the float, then it can pay to tie direct to a 14 barbless and really lay into them once they are hooked, lifting them straight to hand, as opposed to netting them. My 64 lb off the Eden comprised nearly all dace, and that will give you some idea of the potential that can be reached with these fish.

As the river runs off and my swim changes, the fish may well move out, and if I'm faced with a cast of more than three or four rod lengths I may often opt for a waggler, but still feed heavily with groundbait and casters. The name of the game, when fishing tidal waters, is keeping in touch with the fish. The river changes by the minute, and so do the fishes' movements. Reading the river is all important, and on these venues your swim can explode into life at any stage of the tide. If you've laid your trap for them, then you should have a chance at some stage of holding them long enough to build a weight.

10 Swimfeeders

Mike Winney

Mike Winney is a 30 year old angling writer from Yorkshire, at present living in the Midlands. Mike has fished four first division Nationals for North Yorks and South Durham and has won money on most of the major match waters in this country and in Ireland. Happiest when he is fishing the lead or the feeder, Mike came to the conclusion some time ago that his match fishing would benefit if he stuck to what he enjoyed and, as a result, he now fishes venues where big fish are likely to score and the lead and feeder more likely to produce. Having said that, Mike also owns an extensive collection of floats which see the light of day from time to time.

Educated at Fettes College, Edinburgh, he soon realized that his only interests lay in fishing and writing, and is now in the enviable position of being able to combine the two for most of his time, and get paid for it.

Mike's big fish to date include eight roach over 2 lb and a chub an ounce short of 5 lb. He has yet to catch a bream over 6 lb, despite having once spent six days at an Irish lakeside which resulted in one bite—a massive bream, as he later found out, which was lost after 20 minutes.

Mike has won matches on the feeder on the Tees, Swale, Yorkshire Ouse, and the Trent, and has been placed on the Severn, Thames and Avon, waters which he is currently coming to terms with as a newcomer to the Midlands circuit.

The swimfeeder revolution is here to stay, there can be little doubt about that, and many forward thinking anglers have swallowed their prejudices and have learnt to handle the method and put it in its true perspective. It was a while before its devastating effect truly dawned on me and such was the impact that I devoted all my practice sessions to fishing the feeder under all conditions. In that initial burst of enthusiasm I didn't iron out all the wrinkles, but it was enough to convince me that if it was a 'feeder job' then I could approach the match with confidence. What is more, I enjoy fishing the feeder and that has a lot to do with it. Fish it with the attitude 'I'll probably catch' and you probably will; fish it with the attitude 'This is the method and I will catch for certain' and you have a head start.

'Ban the feeder' they cry, but surely that's what they said about the swingtip when it first started to make a big impact. The feeder, like the tip, isn't a magic formula—but it is an improvement. True enough, anyone with just a basic knowledge of angling could cast out a feeder on the Severn in summer and he would probably beat the skilful angler at the next peg, if he fished the float. Put that same beginner next to someone who really knows what he is doing on the feeder and the result would be a massacre.

Any match angler who thinks he can ignore the feeder is only kidding himself; as long as it remains a legitimate means of catching fish, then it is a must in his repertoire and, to derive any benefit from it, he must understand its mechanics. It isn't enough to carry a couple round in his basket, to be put on when all else fails.

Why it works
Before we look at the mechanics of feeder fishing, it would be best to see why it works so well. The feeder makes everyone who uses it properly an accurate groundbaiter every single cast, providing he can cast consistently to the same spot. It also makes the angler feed on a regular basis, a factor which is the key to success in many rivers. Fishing the float or the straight leger, the angler forgets to feed or he feeds too much, or too little. This is where the advantages stop. From then on the angler has to be every bit as skilful as the next man if he wishes to build up a winning weight, or enough to get him in the frame. Bear in mind that every time he reels in, which should be frequently, he is filling the feeder and putting it back in his swim. To fish it properly it is essential to feed a regular, measured amount; the fact that his hookbait is lying amongst a carpet of free offerings is the icing on the cake. It has to be the ultimate combination of accurate feeding on a regular basis and the hookbait right in the middle of it. Having established that the feeder does work, and why, the match angler then has to establish when, and how.

When to use the feeder

This question could be answered simply by saying any time, on moving waters. That, however, would be glib, for whereas it may always provide a few fish, there are plenty of venues where it is not as effective as the float. The Trent, for example, will turn up fish at every peg on the feeder, but if there aren't enough big fish feeding, then the float or pole will be quicker every time. In a Trent swim, where there is a head of bream or chub, then I doubt very much if I would even put up a float rod. Even on matches where the target weight is 3-4 lb then the feeder has to give you a better-than-even chance of picking up one bonus fish and a few bits. The big Yorkshire rivers, the Ouse and Ure respond well to the 'pot'. The depth and flow are such that it is hard to groundbait with any degree of accuracy at a distance, and the certain knowledge that your bait is on the bottom, surrounded by loose feed, is a great confidence booster. The other obvious match waters where the feeder is a must are the Severn, Avon, Witham (when it's pulling), Tees, Swale, Thames, Ribble, Broads' rivers, in fact anywhere there is a good head of chub, barbel or bream.

As for stillwaters, I'm not yet convinced that a swimfeeder is the answer. It may well catch but there is no flow to disperse the feed. As most match anglers are capable of using a catapult to cover an area with a pattern in a short time, that is a better method than using a swimfeeder to lay down a bed of bait over a period of maybe half an hour, with all the surface splashes that this would involve. It may be adequate for pleasure anglers, but I have yet to be convinced that it would be effective in matches. If you don't believe me, imagine the effect on a shoal of stillwater bream of a feeder being dragged through their midst after you strike at a 'liner'. Miss a couple of bites with a ⅜ oz bomb and you've got problems enough.

Tackle

There are dozens of brands of feeders on the market; some of them have no application for sensible anglers, others will do the job perfectly. There are basically three types; block-end; open-end and the small Feederlinks. The block and open-ended feeders come in three sizes – small,

Mike Winney with a catch of lower Severn bream . . . taken on a swimfeeder rig (© Mike Winney)

medium and large. The feederlinks and the small and medium versions of the block and open-ended can be fished close in with your normal leger rods with a slight increase in reel line strength. I would choose a 4 lb reel line. Others will tell you that you can get away with 3 lb, but this is cutting it a bit fine if there's a lot of casting and retrieving involved.

It's a different picture altogether if you're fishing the big block-end feeders. However uncouth and ungainly they look when they hit the water, these are the real match winners because they can get 1½ gallons of feed down on that river bed in five hours, and that sort of heavy feeding really gets the fish lined up in your swim. But your tackle does have to be strong, positive, with no frills to impede a steady rhythm. The scale of the tackle required would frighten off a lot of anglers. - those to whom it would be foreign to fish with powerful rods, 5-7 lb line and possibly no bite indicator, save your rod end.

There are a few feeder rods currently on the market and some of the rods designed for other uses suit heavy feeder work. What you are looking for is a rod about 11ft 6 in with a straight through action. The best rings that money can buy should be fitted - any chinks in their armour will soon be detected by the hard work they will be subject to. My two heavy feeder rods are cut down from heavy float rods, one has a small donkey top spliced in and the other has just the rod end as a bite indicator.

The next essential is to have a good reel, since fishing the feeder will test it to the fullest. Personally, I would recommend the ABU Cardinal 44 Express, some may prefer the Mitchell or even one of the bigger ABUs. Whatever you choose, only the best in your eyes, will be good enough. Use anything from 4-7 lb line strength - weaker line will give you problems. Hook lengths can and indeed should be a bit lighter.

Another necessity for fishing the big feeder in fast water is a good, strong, bankstick - 6 ft isn't too long if you want your rod well up in the air, to keep the line off the water and to stop the feeder dragging.

Feeder rigs
The motto for this is the simpler the better!

The feeder isn't like float fishing, where you are constantly trying to find the depth and speed at which the fish want the bait. The feeder predetermines all that for you. It gets the bait on the bottom and that's where the fish will *have* to feed if they want a share of the action. If you read anything else into the method, then you're making heavy weather of it and confusing the issue. There are few refinements you can make. Apart from varying the length between the hook and feeder and the obvious change in hook size and strength of hook length, there aren't many options open. Once barbel and chub start having a go,

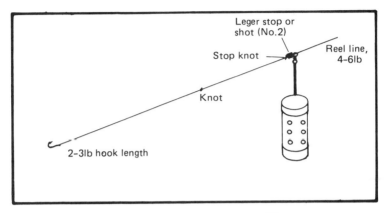

Fig. 10.1 Terminal set-up suitable for heavy reel lines

your main worry will be having enough stamina to keep them coming!

One of the main problems anglers have is how to attach the feeder to the line and the subsequent terminal tackle set-up. This often results in a lot of tangles, kinks and breakages. The simplest and most effective methods are shown on this page.

Figure 10.3 shows a close-up of a big block-end feeder suitable for the Trent or Severn, where a fast emptying rate is essential to build up a swim. It is also tangle-proof, providing you add enough weight to the feeder to hold the bottom. The 10 lb line from the swivel to the feeder is encased in a length of valve rubber. This link is the key to trouble-free feeder fishing; it shields the bottom half of the

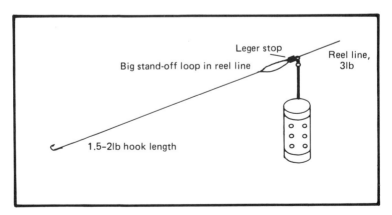

Fig. 10.2 Terminal set-up for light reel lines

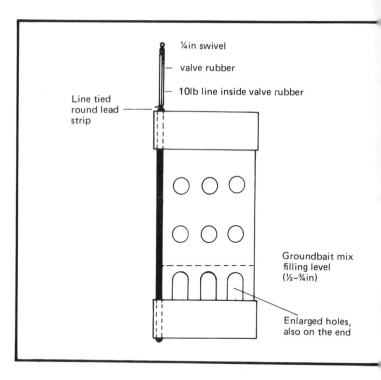

Fig. 10.3 Big block-end for Severn, Trent,, etc., with modifications

top swivel as well as the knot at the feeder. It's neater than a system of clips and links and there's nothing that can go wrong with it. The only disadvantage is that to remove it from the line you have to break down the terminal tackle, but that's a minor inconvenience.

In Fig. 10.1 the reel line simply goes through the eye of the swivel and is stopped by a small shot or leger stop, which in turn is held secure by a small loop knot. As this knot weakens the line, however, this set-up is best used with heavy line. For weaker lines, the set-up in Fig. 10.2 would be advisable, with the loop providing a stand-off link for the hook length. The whole purpose is to stop the line wrapping round any part of the terminal tackle, so that when a fish takes the bait, it doesn't feel undue resistance. Possibly the best way to illustrate the most effective ways of fishing the feeder to win, is to describe a couple of matches in detail, one on the Trent and one on the Severn.

A feeder match on the Trent

The Trent will be *the* river for the feeder during the next few years, because of its exploding chub population. There is only one way to approach the Trent if you want to perform well and that's by an *all out attack*. First of all, you'll need plenty of bait—ten pints of maggots, four pints of casters and a couple of pints of hemp. You'll also need 5 lb of groundbait. If that seems excessive, bear in mind that ten fills of a big feeder take care of a pint of maggots and a feeding chub can easily eat upwards of half a pint of feed. The casters, hemp and groundbait can all be mixed together in a big bowl. My block-end feeders for the Trent and Severn have been modified to allow an immediate release of bait once the feeder has settled. The enlarged holes at the bottom are sealed up with half an inch of groundbait, casters and hemp, packed in tightly with the maggots jammed in on top. As soon as the feeder hits the bottom, the groundbait and casters disintegrate in the flow and the big holes soon disperse the maggots – to coin a well-known advertising slogan, the maggots 'simply flood through'.

To start a match on the Trent, I pick a line further out than anyone else is fishing, in fact, the further out the better, and it gives me all that line of the river to myself as well, which I can fish quite comfortably with the tackle I have.

My feeder will have up to 1 oz of extra lead in it, my reel line will be no less than 5 lb and my hook length probably 3 lb, and I'd start off on a No. 14 with two maggots. The first priority then is to get some bait down and establish a swim, not to get bites. If I do get bites at this stage it's just an added bonus. As soon as the whistle goes, I'm in and out with that feeder every minute, till I've got about 1½ pints down on the deck. In between every cast, I also catapult a ball of groundbait out, rock hard and full of casters and hemp. This also helps to build up the swim and providing I judge the flow and depth correctly, it ensures a continuous stream of bait down that line and it also feeds off the gudgeon and smaller fish. It's chub and bream I'm after and once they move in, I wouldn't expect to be catching anything else.

You'll need a long rod rest for this game, as the rod needs to be well off the water, at an angle of no less than 45 degrees. When the bites come, they are liable to be drop back bites, as the fish pick up the bait and move downsteam. This will nudge the feeder from its anchorage and the rod will drop back. In fact, the first signs you get will be that the tip will move down first and then drop back quickly. An immediate response is necessary. Some days all that is needed to make contact is simply to lift the rod and ease into the fish, which may well have hooked itself. This happens if you are using a stiff rod end as a bite indicator, when the fish can hook itself against the resistance. With a soft quivertip, the reverse will happen and the tip will often bounce the bait out of its mouth, once that feeder moves. If positive bites aren't forthcoming, then I scale up to an 18 and single maggot. If this doesn't improve matters and I'm still getting bites and missing them, then I would stand up and touch leger. Sometimes, the effect of this can be staggering, believe me.

It's hard work fishing the feeder like this for five hours, and it's important to get into a steady work pattern, and also to have your kit laid out properly. To start with, you don't want your keepnet anywhere near where you will be swinging and loading your feeder, as a hook caught in a net can waste time and throw you off your routine just when you start catching. Your basket needs to be on firm ground with your groundbait bowl and maggot bowl side by side, in front of you. Your towel needs to be handy, as do your forceps and disgorger. These are all small points, but if you are at all interested in time and motion you will see that you can cut down 5 seconds each time you load and cast your feeder, which soon adds up.

My experiences with the feeder on the Trent have taught me that the longer the match progresses, the better my swim will be. My first hour is often blank but that doesn't bother me unduly. As soon as I get that tell-tale rattle of a big fish, then I know I have a better than even chance of keeping them coming. Sometimes you can get bites and fish at every cast, using maybe a 14 and a double maggot when suddenly the bites tail off. This is when you have to make a quick decision – have the fish gone, or are they hook shy, or shy of two maggots?

My first move, in this situation would be to whip on an 18 with the feeder and fish single maggot. More often than not this is all it takes to have them coming back again. I've also found that the best way to hook fish on an 18 with the feeder is to dispense with the quivertip and fish the rod end, simply letting the fish hook themselves, which they do quite happily. There is no need to strike either, since the fish are used to finding single maggots from the feeder, so they pick up yours, move downstream and the resistance of the rod end simply stabs the small hook home. All you have to do is lift the rod and you're in business. If you strike, you'll probably tear the hook through the bream's or chub's lip.

Contrary to popular opinion, I don't believe that fish, once they are feeding on the bottom of the Trent, get line shy – they may become wary of large hooks or multiple maggots, but 3 lb line offers no deterrent to quality roach. I've caught them on the Trent on 7 lb line direct to a 10 and single maggot, and plenty of times on my normal chub rig of a 14 and 3 lb. Hook size is the key to bites; everything else must be tackled up with the flow of the river and the heavy work involved taken into consideration. The fish don't care if you use a 3 lb reel line or 5 lb, so why make things difficult for yourself? Tackle up so that you are fishing confidently.

Trent tackle list:
    Two feeder rods (spliced in quiver and rod end)
    Biggest feeder, plus 1 oz lead
    5 lb reel line, 3 lb hook length
    Hooks 14-18
    Long bankstick
    Bait: 10 pints maggots, 4 pints casters, 5 lb groundbait,
        2 pints hemp
    Target weight: 10-15 chub, bream or carp (14 lb to get
        into the frame)

A feeder match on the Severn
This is where the revolution began and the potential of the feeder was first realized. Southerners and Yorkshiremen will argue that they have used the feeder with great success for years but that isn't the point in question. The Severn proved that if there's a large head of fish, a large amount of bait was required to keep them happy, and the big feeders did this job accurately and with deadly effect. Such was the impact of the feeder that anyone seen fishing the float on the middle Severn in summer was regarded as an 'also ran' and they generally were.

The match I will describe took place in Bewdley in August. My peg was 3 ft deep and moving through. At first glance it looked a no hoper, but to the keen Severn matchman, it's a flyer. As usual, the bait list was big – 2 gallons of maggots and maybe a few casters to offer a bit of variety if they go off. The quarry for most of the time was barbel with maybe a few chub. Tackle: 2 heavy feeder rods; 6-8 lb reel line; one rod with the reel line straight through to a No. 10 hook and the other with a 5 lb hook length and a No. 14 hook. I also needed a big rod rest to keep the bulk of the line off the water and the tackle laid out in an orderly fashion, with my maggot bowl between my feet. The feeder had the holes enlarged to allow a quick escape of bait and it was occasionally necessary to add some lead to the feeder to stop it rolling. The Severn is now so heavily fished with the feeder that the barbel and chub respond immediately to the splash in the swim. Within seconds of your first cast you could find yourself into a barbel. In fact that was exactly what happened in the first match I fished on the Severn. No sooner had I engaged the bale arm and put the rod on the rest, than the rod end was pulled viciously round. What a baptism!

The faster and shallower the swim, the more chance you have of scoring heavily with the barbel. I normally start off with a No. 10 direct to 6 lb line with a single maggot as hookbait. As soon as the feeder is empty – which can be as little as 20 seconds in a fast swim – you have to think about reeling in and reloading. The bites I look for should come within 10 seconds of the feeder settling, if I have to wait a few minutes for a bite, then I'm struggling. The only answer is to keep casting and reloading every thirty seconds to build up a big blanket of bait to stir the barbel and chub into feeding. I sometimes also scale down to a 14 hook and a longer tail. If the flow is washing the feed downstream too quickly, then my hookbait is nowhere near the feed and even though I might be picking up the odd fish, I've no chance of winning. I look for about 35 lb in the first two hours and if my catch rate doesn't look like giving me that sort of score, then I'm only making up the numbers.

The great thing is to keep going, even if the bites stop altogether. There's nothing worse than leaving your feeder in for, say, 5 or even 10 minutes, hoping to pick up a stray fish. It has to be a full five hours attack, with a continual stream of maggots going down the same line all the time. On occasions when the bites are shy and not developing, then it certainly pays to touch leger with the feeder. The difference this can make, as on the Trent, can be surprising. Fishing the feeder on the Severn can be something of an endurance test, even 1½ barbel in fast flow can feed three times their own size and amassing a big weight requires a lot of physical strength. One small point – if you are touch legering, don't wrap the line around your finger, not unless you want it amputated. Barbel when they feel the hook can, and often do, drag rods off their rests with comparative ease.

Feeder tackle for the Severn:
  Two heavy duty rods (no quivertips);
  Biggest block-end feeders with enlarged holes
  7 lb line straight through to a 10, and 5 lb bottom to a
    14 (forged hooks)
  Large bankstick rod rest
  Bait: 12-16 pints of maggots, 2 pints casters
  Target weight for Bewdley: 75 lb to get in the frame,
    90 lb to win

11 Pole Fishing

John Carding

Born and educated in London, where he now lives, 27 year old advertising director John is a regular contributor to *Angler's Mail* and *Coarse Fisherman* and has two previous books to his credit, *Continental Pole Fishing* and *Match Fishing*. A qualified NFA/NAC angling instructor, he devotes a lot of time to coaching youngsters in the south, as well as giving talks to clubs and forums.

Currently a member of the highly successful London based 279 AC, John has just put together his most rewarding season, finishing fourth in the prestigious Southern All-Stars Top 20 League and coming third overall in the two leg Southern All-Stars versus Greenways (Midland) Top 20, winning his section on the Warwickshire Avon at Evesham and on the Lee at Fishers Green. John doesn't fish one water exclusively and picked up money on the Kentish Rother, Royal Military Canal, Thames, Medway, Wallers Haven, Lee and Warwickshire Avon and various still waters during the 1977-78 season.

Though well qualified to write on pole fishing – he made several visits to France to study the method closely and has written a book on the subject – he is also an accomplished all rounder, as his results in the past two seasons will testify.

Introduction
The match angling fraternity in this country is currently showing a greater interest than ever before in the techniques and tackle used by their continental counterparts. In the past it was the exceptional British matchman who sat in front of a forest of poles. Nowadays, poles are as common as rods and reels in many matches, if not more so. Although the popular misconception that existed a few years ago, that the pole was solely a weapon for catching small fish and nothing else, seems to have waned, the basics of pole fishing still remain a mystery to a large percentage of match anglers.

I'm certain that a lot of the problems that exist are often caused by a simple lack of understanding, and with so few knowledgeable anglers passing information along it is of little surprise that what is basically an easy technique is shrouded in confusion. The tackle trade have been slow to learn and instruct their customers, and the lack of understanding in combination with some of the tackle on offer, is hardly the ideal situation.

Choice of poles
So what, then, is the right tackle to buy? First of all, the pole itself. I suggest that you should always go for a rigid, take-apart pole. The stiffest you can get. Soft telescopic poles have only one main use and that's for greased line fishing for bleak (see chapter 12), a technique that is British in origin.

As well as being as rigid as possible, the pole you purchase should be as light as possible, and carbon fibre would be the obvious choice. It's strong, light and rigid. However, if you are going to use a long pole, you would have to be thinking in terms of paying in the region of £300 for carbon fibre, and I'm sure for the vast majority that sort of expenditure would not be worthwhile. But when you get up to 27 ft poles, carbon is the only answer, as even the lightest glass is far too heavy to do the job effectively.

Stiff, take-apart, fibre glass poles are the ideal for the majority of anglers, and you should bear in mind that it is cheaper in the long run to start off with a 27 ft pole and work up to using all the sections. Having the extra length available from the start of your pole fishing is by far the best way to learn.

Which pole to select from the large range on offer? It's obviously a personal thing; I've used two Garbolino 'Leader' poles (21 ft and 27 ft) for the past two years and they do everything I demand of a pole. Why don't I use carbon fibre? Well, I've used carbon poles and there are situations where they offer a distinct advantage, especially at distance, and there is a good chance that I will get one in the near future. However, there is one big plus in favour of the Garbolinos and that is, I'm used to them! Like a float rod that you have used for several years, they become an extension of your arm and a familiar rod is more effective than a brand new model.

One of the dangers of modern match angling is that

'Apart from weight and rigidity, the other consideration when choosing a pole is that the ferrules should come apart easily'
(© Jim Lauritz)

people swap and change too often, dedicated followers of fashion, if you like. A pole is no different; and providing it suits you, there is no advantage gained in changing to the latest model every year.

Apart from weight and rigidity, the other consideration when choosing a pole, is that the ferrules must come apart easily. Sticking occurs usually with poles in which the male and female ferrule fit together in a parallel sleeve. For the joint to come apart easily, the male ferrules should have a very, very slight taper on the last couple of inches.

If the pole that you already own has ferrules that stick, I suggest you first try scraping off any paint and varnish which may have been left on by the manufacturer; fine sandpaper should do the job. If this still doesn't solve the problem, use a heavier grade sandpaper and start by taking a fraction off the male ferrule. Keep testing until you get it right and be careful not to take too much off. A loose ferrule is worse than one that sticks.

Balanced pole tackle
The crook attachment, used in conjunction with the elastic shock absorber, undoubtedly offers a great advantage to

the angler when using delicate tackle. The elastic absorbs any initial pull when a decent fish is hooked and therefore protects the fragile tackle. I'm sure that most of you already understand (although some may not) that pole gear, in particular the elastic shock absorber, has to be balanced with the correct main line and hook length or you are wasting the advantage it offers you. Balance – it's the key to the whole thing. The only way to be sure you have the correct strength of elastic for each occasion is to equip yourself with all of the four breaking strains and match them with the rest of your terminal tackle. The four strengths available are extra-fine, fine, medium and stout. Extra-fine should be employed with a ¾ lb main line, ½ lb hook length and very light floats. The fine is the next grade up and should be coupled with 1 lb main line and ¾ lb hook lengths and slightly heavier floats. Medium is for 1-2 lb main line and corresponding hook lengths. The stout elastic is pretty powerful stuff and should be used when there are snags or weed in the swim or where quality fish can be expected. Hook lengths of 2 lb should balance out with the stout elastic. There is little point in using elastic which is either overpowered or underpowered, unbalanced tackle prevents you using your pole to its full capacity.

Choice of pole floats and weights

Such is the variety of pole floats on offer that many newcomers to pole fishing fall down at this hurdle – dozens of different floats are just not necessary. Most of the top continental anglers carry anything up to say 150 winders, with a different rig on each, but they will usually have no more than three or four types of floats, in varying sizes. I only carry four patterns of pole floats (see Fig. 11.1) in a variety of sizes and I would certainly advise budding pole anglers to do the same. Float 'A' is the type I use for still or slow pace water. As you can see from the diagram, it is not unlike a stick float in shape, thin at the bottom and getting wider at the top, where there is a wire insert. Because of its shape, it can easily be worked through a swim, rather like a stick float. I carry a range of five of these floats, taking between one No. 4 and 1½ BB, bulk capacity. Bear in mind that that is the capacity, not the final shotting pattern. Float 'B' is for use in still water only, particularly if the swim is deep or conditions are

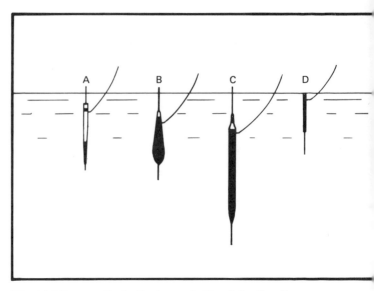

Fig. 11.1 Range of pole floats carried by John Carding

choppy. It's thick bottomed and this gives it the stability I require to present my bait in adverse conditions. I use four of these floats and they range from 1BB to 3BB capacity. Float 'C' is similar to 'A' in shape, but has a large cylindrical body of hollow balsa; this gives a maximum shot carrying capacity per float. I'll use these in fast and/or deep water and they range from 1AAA to 1 swan. Once again, I carry four in the range. They are not a common design, but they are available from specialist shops. In fact they are designed by the Frenchman Marcel Despres and sold under that name.

Float 'D' is completely different from the other three types. Whilst they are made from light-grade balsa and wire and all shop bought, 'D' is a home made job of peacock quill and wire. I have these in three sizes, taking between one No. 8 and three No. 8 capacity. As you can see from the diagram, the float lacks the wire insert at the tip that is a feature of the other three. I shot it so that the top is virtually level with the surface and find it ideal for fishing sub-surface for bleak and other small species. By sub-surface I mean at depths of 2-4 feet. I usually fish it with a string of small shot between sizes 10-13. These floats also do a good job in extreme shallows, waters of no more than 18 inches, where perhaps gudgeon are the prime target.

'Probably the one aspect of pole fishing, as the Continentals apply it, that still has not yet been fully exploited in this country, is their approach to feeding a swim.' John Carding seen here groundbaiting continental style (© Jim Lauritz)

All my floats carry a tiny eyelet near the top of the body. By passing your line through this and using a fine rubber at the base of the wire float stem, the float can be held back without causing it to rise up in the water. This is simply because the float is being pulled from the side rather than from the top, causing very little upward pressure to be transmitted.

The most important thing to do when using the majority of pole floats, sub-surface rigs being the obvious exception, is to plumb the depth of your swim. Only when you have done this should you make a final choice of float. In the majority of cases, I use continental style 'Olivetti' leads, in conjunction with small shot for my pole floats. The Olivetti leads are perfect for bottom fishing. They are designed for fast entry into the water and work more effectively than bunched shot. They are also far less prone to tangle than split shot.

Continental Groundbaiting

Probably the one aspect of pole fishing, as the continentals apply it, that still has not yet been fully exploited in this country, is their approach to feeding a swim. I have watched Frenchmen hurl in two dozen grapefruit sized balls of groundbait almost at their feet and then, when the waves have barely subsided, snatch a fish, first cast.

The method in their madness, is to create a false bed to their swim, allowing the thousands of jokers packed into the huge balls of feed, to escape in a continuous stream. Make no mistake about its potential for this country. In the 1978 England v. France friendly international, fished on the Thames, each member of the French team must have gone through 1½ gallons of neat jokers on a river that many top anglers have said just doesn't respond to the joker and bloodworm, and on which heavy groundbaiting is the kiss of death. Needless to say the French won the match.

But the French certainly can't be accused of wearing blinkers, for they are studying our methods and the way we score with squatts and pinkies. As their matches only last for two hours, then this obviously influences the way they attack their swim. It is one area, however, in which I feel we have a great deal to learn.

The continentals don't always 'fill it in'. If the swim has a weedy bottom, they will introduce a light mix and try and take their fish in mid-water. Obviously the continental style of groundbaiting won't work on every venue. In fact I'm sure I've come unstuck a few times by trying it.

The pole is undoubtedly a winning method on the right venue on the day. Keep it in perspective and don't be afraid to use it—it could put you in the frame.

12 Bleak Fishing

John Carding

Introduction

Twenty-five years ago, bleak fishing as a method was virtually non-existent in this country. Bleak that were caught came more by accident and were regarded as a nuisance by the majority of anglers. The suggestion that you could win matches with them and that you could set your stall out to catch them was treated with little regard.

For far too long bleak were treated as a dirty word in match fishing circles and I have always failed to understand the reason for this. The whole idea of competitive angling, as I understand it, is that it's my job to catch the fish in my swim on the day. If these fish turn out to be bleak, then it's bleak I'll fish for.

Many anglers who, in the past, accepted bleak as 'reasonable game', failed to fish for them with any real thought. As recently as the mid-sixties I can remember many anglers fishing for bleak in matches using conventional float fishing set-ups, and for every fish caught a dozen bites were missed and another dozen not seen.

Fortunately, the situation has now changed and bleak fishing has become a sophisticated and essential part of the modern match angler's repertoire of skills. It would be true to say that a good 'bleaker' is in his element when the big fish aren't feeding – it is on such days that the competent bleak angler can destroy the rest of the field. A classic example of this was the 1100 peg 1973 Bass Charrington Gala, fished on the Welland between Spalding and Crowland. The river was off-form and the bream just didn't settle to feed. Doncaster matchman, Roger Frith, shook the country's match angling fraternity by putting 21 lb 9 oz on the scales – made up almost entirely of bleak.

Certainly though, bleak fishing has another great attraction and that is that it is team fishing. When bleak are in the swim the efficient bleaker is on a certain backing weight. In modern team events, fished on sections and points, competence at bleaking by team members I'd regard not only as an advantage, but a necessity.

A small – but section-winning – catch taken on a day when it was necessary to scale down the basic rig to catch shy biting fish (© Jim Lauritz)

The techniques needed to catch bleak are relatively simple, but even the easiest of techniques need practice and none more than 'bleaking'. Fishing on the surface at close range is without doubt the most specialized and efficient method for building up a weight of bleak. It is a method which can produce 200 fish plus per hour and this is the approach I want to look at in depth.

The pole(s)

If you want to catch several fish a minute, which, with surface bleaking, should be your aim, the type of pole employed is an important consideration. The pole selected needs to become an extension of your arm so you don't even need to think about it. The first thought when selecting your pole for this style is that it must be the lightest possible. A low diameter handle is also a great asset when you consider that you could be casting, unhooking and rebaiting possibly over 200 times an hour.

I carry two poles for surface bleaking, both soft and whippy, the Shakespeare Polyestal telescopic 1091/345 (11 ft 3 in) and 1080/450 (14 ft 7 in). The shorter of the two is slightly stiffer since the distance and effort required to cast and strike is less. For speed in unhooking and rebaiting, the line is fixed at a foot less than the pole length, enabling you to swing your fish to hand.

The basic rig

All my surface rigs are stored on winders and are made up of three different types of line. A typical rig for use when the bleak are feeding well in the top 6 in of water would consist of the main line of 2.5 lb attached to the top of the pole. Next is 3 ft 6 in of 'invisible' mending thread, and finally, a 6 in trace of 2 lb to a size 16 barbless hook (Fig. 12.1). The float is fixed by two rubbers 4 ft up the line. The type I use for surface fishing are small – 2 in long – plastic 'duckers' (Fig. 12.2). I find these ideal for the job, which is to provide just enough weight for a controlled cast and not to act as a bite indicator.

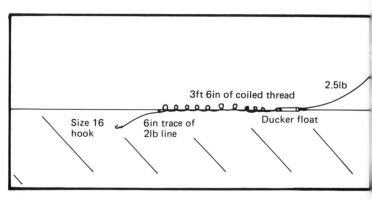

Fig. 12.1 Basic surface bleaking rig

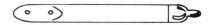

Fig. 12.2 Plastic ducker float (actual size)

The most important part of the rig is the 'invisible' mending thread. The type I use can be purchased on cotton reels from an appropriate shop for about 12p for a hundred yards. The brand that is silvery-white in colour and coils easily is the best – it is its coiling ability that is crucial, the coils being your bite indicator!

Placing the 'ducker' float 4 ft from the hook, you then 'crimp' the thread between your thumb and first fingernail, drawing it down from the float to the start of the trace. Providing you have the right type of thread, this will give you a pig's tail effect and this is what you watch for bite indication. Its advantages are that it offers less resistance to a taking fish and it is far more sensitive an indicator than a float.

The final touch to this rig is treating the thread with silicon-muslin. This will make it stand up in the water. The last 6 in of the line – the trace – should sink, and you can aid this by rubbing it gently with mud from the bankside.

Variations on the basic rig
The rig described above is only the basic set-up for when the fish are feeding well. Greased line fishing for bleak has a far greater application than this one rig. On a good day when the bleak are coming every cast and showing no hesitation in taking the hookbait, the rig described is perfect. The only modification I would make if the fish are coming really well is to move my float nearer the hook, leaving less line to pick up and hopefully, therefore, hook more fish as a result. You should always bear in mind, however, that the nearer the float is to the hook, the quicker the strike must be.

There have been occasions when I have found that scaling right down to a ¾ lb bottom and a size 24 barbless has been the answer to catch shy surface feeding bleak. This type of tackle is required most frequently when the water is gin-clear and there is no surface ripple. On the day you will need to experiment to find the most productive surface rig.

On the occasions when you are able to use and catch on a 16 hook and 2 lb trace, you should be on your way to a big bag, but remember that this isn't the only time greaseline fishing will put you in the money.

The frequency of bites can sometimes be increased with a surface rig by splashing your tackle down onto the water. There are two theories why this works; one is that the bleak associate surface noise with feed going in and the other is that they think the splash is another bleak 'flipping' on the surface. Conversely, it often pays to adopt a gentle approach, dropping your tackle lightly on the surface.

At times a small split shot can also be added to get the terminal tackle down, if the fish have dropped lower in the water. Another occasion when the addition of a couple of No. 10s is helpful is when an upstream wind holds the line and prevents the bait sinking at the correct speed.

Tough hook maggots, hooks and 'flicking off'
Maggots are by far the best hookbait for bleak and should be the toughest you can find. The older and thicker-skinned the maggot is the better, because then it will last for several fish before you have to change it. Bleak will still take it even when it has been reduced to a skin, and you can keep fishing as long as the bites still come frequently. The only disadvantage of this time saving tactic is the habit of the bleak blowing the maggot up the line, causing you to take more time to replace it.

The problem can be solved by using the right sort of hook; by this I mean not so much size but the pattern. An eyed hook is essential as the eye will prevent the maggot from moving onto the line. Another great time saver is flicking your fish off instead of stopping to unhook each one. This is quite simple with practice – as the bleak is swung in the line is caught 6 in above the fish with the little finger of the hand uppermost, the hand is then turned sharply over and off comes the fish. Unfortunately, one fish in six is hooked in the lower jaw, these can't be flicked off and you will have to take the hook out in the normal way.

Some final tips
Once you have decided to go for bleak in a match, the first priority is to have your keepnet positioned correctly, in such a way that the fish that are flicked off will land in it. The top ring of the net should be at least 22 in diameter to

provide a large target area. If it doesn't make the fish wary you will find that you operate better standing, which will enable you to wear an apron - a great time saver. For hookbaits I like a selection of new and old maggots of various colours—despite what I said earlier about old maggots lasting for several fish, sometimes the bleak want soft, new ones. For feeders I use casters, pinkies and assorted maggots. This variety of feed confuses the bleak and they don't then fall into a routine of accepting feed at a certain rate of fall and making your hookbait stand out. If the bleak respond well and I'm chasing a decent weight, I'll feed between 6 and 12 feeders every cast that results in a fish. Too many maggots and the bleak boil on the surface and become too hard to hook; too few and they will move off. Again, experience is the only answer to the question of how much to put in.

Although time is all-important when bleak fishing, establishing a simple, smooth rhythm is the first priority - experience and confidence in your approach will eventually give you a high speed.

13 Casters

If you had to name one bait that has transformed the 'trim' of the major match venues in this country, then that award would doubtless go to the caster.

Of course casters have been used on the hook for many years. The late, great Sam Buxton who ruled the Witham many years since, knew all about them, but only as a change bait. The concept of feeding large amounts into the river and fishing the caster on the hook didn't really come about until the Lancashire invasion of the Trent in the mid-sixties, when the caster revolution really took place, and the Trent maggot men could only look on bemused, as week after week they saw their money head off west !

The implications of the changes this bait could make on a river just weren't fully realized at the time. After the Lancashire men, who pioneered caster fishing, had cleaned up on the river, anglers began to switch to casters on other venues, with outstanding results.

The Nene, Witham, Severn, and Welland all responded so well to the bait that the humble maggot took a back seat. It soon became apparent that not only would the caster catch roach, but chub, barbel, bream, in fact there wasn't a fish swimming that couldn't be educated to accept the bait, and the beauty of it was that it was the better stamp of fish that fell to the caster. The next breakthrough was on the Fen bream rivers. 'Caster pie' became the in feed. Softer groundbait, packed with casters, became the accepted feeding recipe for the bream, for not only did the mix break up on impact and cause less disturbance, but the feed-to-bread ratio could be increased to such an extent that feeding squatts and pinkies became a thing of the past.

The results on the Welland, Witham and Nene speak for themselves and stand as testimony to the effect casters in the feed had. As it was, the only stretch of water where this tactic just didn't work was the massive Relief Channel at Downham Market. The reason, quite simply, was that the Northern bream matchmen, mostly from South Yorkshire, rarely fished the channel, as there were so few big events on the water, with the result that the regulars still fed their squatts and fished gozzers, but even that is changing now. Like so many trends in angling, however, there had to be a full swing and in the case of the Witham, Trent and Nene the caster lost its pulling power and the maggot men started to make inroads. This time it was the men from the other side of the Pennines who made the transition. The anglers from Leeds and Bradford ruled again.

Caster preparation
There are several methods of preparing casters and all of them obtain the same end result, clean, fresh, sinking casters.

For an average five hour match you will probably need no less than 4 pints of bait. Bear in mind that to obtain 4 pints of casters, you will need 6 pints of maggots to be on the safe side. Maggots for turning should be bought fresh, the week before the match, on a Thursday or Friday. As soon as you get the maggots, which ideally should be large meat fed maggots, sieve them off and remove all the skins and dirt and place them in clean, fine sawdust, slightly dampened, in a large, open container, such as a biscuit tin or washing up bowl and leave them in a dark room, which has a fairly standard temperature but is not too cool.

On the Tuesday before the match, riddle them again and take off any casters that have turned and any skins. If the sawdust is drying, dampen slightly; this is to ensure that when the maggots really start to turn, they won't be too dry. Excessively dry conditions have the effect of causing them to shrivel and they make poor casters; dampened maggots turn at their leisure and are full bodied and more attractive to fish.

Repeat the same procedure on Wednesday. It's still a bit early to start fridging them, but luckily you will have only had to throw away a handful. By Thursday, however, you will have to start thinking in terms of riddling them off twice a day, to ensure that the casters don't develop too quickly before they can be fridged. When they start turning, place them in an airtight container and place them in the fridge. Friday and Saturday will see the bulk of the maggots turn and these should be added to the ones already in the container, but be sure to let those already fridged 'breathe' for a few minutes every day. At this stage of development casters are still very much living things and need air, as do maggots. They may appear to be fresh, but if they die they will sour inside the shell. You may not be able to tell the difference but the fish will!

The final riddle on Sunday morning should see you achieve your ½ gallon target. If, at the height of summer, you are troubled with 'black fly' in your maggots, then you should really take them out, and the only way to do it is by hand. Black fly casters are black and hard and next to useless as a feed. It's an unavoidable chore, but necessary if you want to ensure a thoroughbred batch.

Caster fishing

Fishing the caster can be a war of nerves! Mostly yours on yourself and if that sounds a bit Irish, then let me explain. Unlike the maggot, which normally produces an immediate response, the converse is true of the caster. It can be two or three hours into a match before the fish really start showing an interest and the temptation is to change over and feed the maggot. That's normally fatal. When casters start to work, then the fish come on strong, you just have to have the confidence that they will start coming. If you set out to fish the caster, then stick with it.

I always remember a story told to me by Mike Winney about the time when Ivan Marks taught him a thing or two on fishing the caster. It's a story worth repeating, to emphasize the confidence required to make full use of the caster.

It was on the river Trent in a mid-week open. Ivan was pegged next to Mike and insisted from the start that the last hour would be golden. Mike fished maggot, Ivan the caster.

With 50 minutes to go, both anglers had about 6 lb and Ivan chattered all the way through the match, insisting that he wasn't worried and that the last hour would belong to him. Mike, having drawn next to Ivan Marks before, was quite used to the 'kidology' and was quite happy just to keep pace. As I said they were dead level with 50 minutes to go. At the weigh in, Mike had 6 lb 2 oz, Ivan, you've guessed, 14 lb 9 oz. Once that better stamp of roach moved in on the bed of bait he had been building up, he caned them, a continual string of fish in the 8-10 oz category, a lesson Mike hasn't forgotten! Casters and hemp are a deadly combination and a cheaper one than just pure caster. Tactics on the Severn, for instance, are to introduce a large quantity of hemp at the start, anything up to three pints and then fish the caster over the top of this bed of feed. It sounds improbable, but I can assure you it works and I would hazard a guess that this ploy will become a lot more widespread in the next few seasons.

14 Maggots, Squatts and Pinkies

The Maggot

The maggot is perhaps the mainstay of every match angler's armoury. Even more so than the caster. Commercial maggots are bred from the fly we know as the bluebottle, and if allowed to feed till they stop they produce a large, fully-fed maggot.

In recent years, colouring maggots has become an important part of the match angler's preparation before a match. Bronze maggots can be obtained by adding a small quantity of chrysodine to the neat maggots, usually a level teaspoonful is enough for half a gallon. Before adding any dye, be sure to sieve and riddle off any sawdust or bran, as this will soak up the dye and weaken the mixture. Bronze maggots in recent years have made a big impact on the Trent, Witham and other major Fenland roach waters.

The next grade of colouring is yellow, and this can be obtained by adding auromine; on certain days roach and bream can show a distinct preference for this lighter colour. Yellow maggots seem to produce well when the water is slightly coloured.

Rhodamine is the third dye in the matchman's armoury, and this gives a red maggot. Roach and especially grayling will on some days come happily to a red maggot to the exclusion of anything else. Some match anglers have also found that bream can be induced to take a red maggot when all other colours have failed. Rhodamine is a particularly vicious dye and maggots do not take that well to it, often expiring within 48 hours if too much is mixed in.

Maggot fishing tends to be heavy, in terms of loose feeding, simply because they have more buoyancy than the caster and to ensure that a good bed of bait is down, it becomes necessary to step up the quantity. Some fish, especially chub and barbel, seem to have an insatiable appetite for the maggot and a single fish can consume upwards of half a pint with ease. The maggot also attracts the smaller fish, bleak, gudgeon, etc., and these fish can dispose of large quantities before they reach the bottom. Maggot fishing on the Trent you will need six pints at least for loose feed, though for slower moving waters like the Avon, four pints should be ample. Maggots make a poor addition to groundbait, by virtue of the fact that their movement inside the mixed ball, even over a period of a few seconds, can be enough to split the ball and cause it to break, often in mid air, with disastrous results.

Pinkies

The pinkie is fast gaining a reputation as a really good change bait when the going starts to get tough. Roach and bream especially can be tempted to feed on pinkies, when the prospect of a maggot can be just too much, especially on quite cold days. The pinkie can be used as a feeder maggot in groundbait for waters where the stamp of fish is small, especially on canals. Pinkies take well to dye and if the going is rough and the bites have dried up a switch to a bronze or red pinkie can often catch you a valuable fish.

They can also be used when worm fishing for bream, especially if the hook size is small, 18-20s, when they can be slipped on the hook over the worm. Not only do they add a bit of colour, but they do help to keep the worm on.

Squatts

The squatt was once the only ingredient in groundbait for bream fishing, and despite the recent popularity of the caster as a feeder the squatt still plays an important part in the match angler's bait list.

The squatt makes such a good feeder maggot for the following reasons. Large quantities can be packed into cereal groundbait without the mix breaking up. Like the caster, once they are on the river bed they stop there, in contrast to the maggot and pinkie, which tend to burrow or move away. They are small, so bream have to work extremely hard to eat enough to fill themselves, and as a consequence are liable to stop in the swim long enough for the angler to build up a weight.

The squatt is the maggot of the housefly, and in summer is bred commercially in large quantities. In winter, however, in some areas, supplies become scarce, due to dealers' reluctance to hold stocks and because there are difficulties involved in breeding them all the year round. But in winter they become a valuable feed (and even hookbait) on canals.

Feeding squatts and fishing pinkies on the hook is a recognized small fish tactic. When the going gets rough a single squatt on a 24 or even a 26 can produce results, and in winter leagues, when fishing for valuable points, it is an ill-equipped team who do not all carry squatts. Better to feed half a dozen squatts than two or three maggots, because a single maggot can well feed one tiny fish off, whereas a small roach or gudgeon can handle a couple of squatts and still be looking for more.

Gozzers

The gozzer maggot is now generally thought of as just a special soft hookbait. In fact the original gozzer maggot was bred from the woodfly and produced a small 'dumpy' shaped maggot, with very thin soft skin, that could be burst easily. The attraction for the bream with the gozzer was that it was soft, and fished over a bed of squatts it provided a tasty alternative.

The modern match angler, may not be able to get a proper 'gozzer' blow, but for this instance we shall discuss obtaining superior hookbait maggots, better known as 'specials'. The process is quite simple. You will need good poultry meat, chicken breast, pigeon or a heart makes an excellent medium.

Preparations, presuming you are in summer, June to September, should commence on the Friday, the week before the match. Wrap the meat up in several loose layers of newspaper, making sure that the meat is accessible to the fly and that at the same time it is well covered, and place the parcel in a biscuit tin or similar, with a layer of bran in the bottom. The container should then be placed somewhere warm and dark, for example a garden shed or garage, with access for flies but not for dogs and cats! The last important step is to cover the top of the container with a piece of plywood, with just a single hole in. The reason is that the type of fly we want to blow on the meat prefers to lay its eggs in the dark. Don't worry about the flies finding the meat – once it starts to go off they can pick up the scent at very long range and will home in on it.

Leave everything for the weekend. On Monday, if everything has gone to plan, on inspecting the meat you should find several clusters of tiny eggs, and this is really quite enough to give ample hookbait for at least two anglers. Replace the meat in the newspaper, for this serves a dual purpose. It stops the smell spreading and it holds in the warmth, which makes the maggots really begin to chew through the feed.

The next step is to make sure that no other flies can lay on the meat, and this can be done by placing a very fine mesh across the top of the container. On Thursday a quick inspection should reveal the tiny maggots burrowing deep into the meat, and even though at this stage of the proceedings they may only be minute you will be amazed at just how much they can grow in the next two days. On the Saturday the specials should be full grown and very little, if any, of the meat will be left. Then simply tip the whole lot out onto a riddle and separate the bones, feathers, etc., sieve them and take off the bran. The neat maggots should then be placed in fresh bran, which can be slightly dampened with water and placed in the fridge till the next day.

Gozzer maggots make a supreme maggot bait for bream, a fish that at times can be so fickle as to be exasperating. When using shop bought maggots on heavily fished bream waters it is quite possible not even to get a bite, or at least not to have one registered. But a change to a soft hookbait can make all the difference, and it is an ill-prepared match angler who doesn't have a few specials with him on the major bream venues like the Welland, Witham or Relief Channel.

15 Other Match Baits

Tares

Tares enjoyed a brief success a few years ago, and whilst they still catch a lot of fish during the summer months, used in conjunction with hemp as feed, anglers are now coming to the conclusion that without the hemp going in, tares are a waiting game. Having said that, I will add that when roach and chub become preoccupied with tares, then the stamp of fish you can expect make it worthwhile.

Tares are pigeon feed, cheap to buy and easy to prepare. A pint of tares should be more than ample for a day's fishing. Though they are basically a hookbait, once fish have arrived in the swim, attracted by hemp, it pays to cut down on feeding the hemp, and instead feed half a dozen tares instead of a large pinch of hempseed.

To prepare, simply soak in water the night before, and if you want them to be dark or black add bicarbonate of soda. In the morning, bring them to the boil and allow to simmer for half an hour. This is usually ample time and they should be checked at ten minute intervals, testing for softness. You don't want the tare to be too well cooked; practice will tell you when they are ready.

For fishing the tare a size 16 or 14 is used, and the seed is simply hooked just below the skin. Don't worry if it looks all wrong on a big hook. I can assure you, once the fish start to get a taste, they won't notice. It pays, wherever possible, if feeding hemp, to bunch your shot as much as possible. If you string them out, you are almost certain to be plagued with shot bites.

Hemp

Along with the caster, luncheon meat and wasp grub, hemp has made a large impact on match fishing. The nickname 'The seeds of death' is appropriate, for when hemp starts to work in a swim, the result can often be a slaughter! Hempseed has been used for years; it was originally introduced into this country by the Poles, after the first world war, and the results they had with it with Thames roach soon attracted a lot of attention.

The original idea was to feed and fish the hemp on the

hook, and whereas this is still a winning method, modern thinking has given the hempseed a new role as the supreme feed in flowing water. Fished in conjunction with tares on the hook and with hemp as the feed, the combination has accounted for a large amount of match-winning nets of fish.

But the new tactic is to feed hemp and often in large quantities, despite the popular conception, and to fish the caster over the layer of hemp. This tactic works well on the Severn and holds roach, chub and barbel in the swim equally well. Introduced in a large quantity, up to 3 pints in one go, it lays down a massive carpet of feed quickly, and where there is a large head of fish, as in the Severn, then it would seem to make sense. Trial and error on your own waters will soon determine how the fish respond to this tactic.

Cooking hemp can be difficult. It seems to vary from batch to batch, but a decent consignment of Chilean hemp should cause no problems. To prepare, usually the night before a match, I place a pint of hemp in two pints of water in a large pan and very slowly bring it to the boil. When it is boiling, I'll switch off, place the lid on and leave it to soak and take in water overnight. Once again (as with tares), if you want your hempseed to be black add a teaspoonful of bicarbonate of soda. In the morning, at least an hour before you have to depart, bring it to the boil again and keep adding water. The hemp should be cooked within an hour, and you can tell when it is ready because it will have swollen, split and the white kernel will be showing. Fished on the hook, or just used as feed, it is a first rate bait and can't be ignored.

Wasp-grub

This is another bait with supposed magical qualities, which match anglers either love or hate. They love it if they have taken the time to go out and get some, and they hate it when the man at the next peg is giving the chub a hammering on it and they haven't got any!

There's an easy answer, set to work in summer and get a supply in. Deep frozen, it is effective for months and gives you a good edge in winter, especially on venues where a couple of chub are worth their weight in gold. Finding wasps' nests is a process of elimination. You can either follow one back to its nest, and that could be a mile away, or go scouting round areas where wasps just love to nest. River banks and sand are favourite haunts. Ditches, hedgerows and refuse tips all have surprising populations, and for some reason so do churchyards (wasps, too). A quiet chat with your local gravedigger can be well worth the time. You can also advertise in the paper, 'Wasps' nests removed free' – that usually does the trick. Whatever your circumstances, there is no excuse for not having any, if you really want some.

Once you have located the nest, the procedure is simple. Wear sensible clothes, overalls, tied at the ankles, gloves over the sleeves and a scarf or balaclava. You'll need a tin of wasp exterminator or *Cymag* if you can get it, and a long handle with a spoon on the end. Quietly approach the nest, place the required dosage on the spoon and scatter it round the entrance. Most powders work on the basis of contact. Once the wasp has walked through the powder, it is pretty well on the way out. As the wasps must use the entrance continually, as they go in and out, they will disperse the poison throughout the nest. Leave for 12 hours to be safe and then carefully dig out. Be sure still to wear some protection, as there may be a few angry stragglers left. One way to find out if the nest is still active or not is to stamp on the ground in the near vicinity; wasps take exception to vibration and will soon be out to investigate if they are in any fit state to do so. The most novel way to deal with wasps' nests that I have ever heard, is to place a blowlamp over the hole of the nest, or rather the flame blowing across the entrance and stamp on the ground and generally disturb the occupants. What happens next, is that the wasps fly out, lose their wings and are rendered harmless. A bit cruel I would have thought, highly effective but possibly rather inefficient in terms of the total population of the nest.

Once you have procured your precious grubs, separate the layers, wrap each one in a couple of sheets of dry newspaper and place in your freezer, taking care to wrap each parcel in airtight polythene bags to prevent contamination. Even though *Cymag* loses its potency after a while, it's not worth risking lives. A couple of nests are usually ample for a five hour match. The best grubs are put to one side as hookbait and the remainder are mulched up and mixed with groundbait – casters can be added as well. The feed can either be introduced in the groundbait or

Southern matchman Jim Carroll with a net of chub caught on wasp-grub (© Jim Lauritz)

it can be fished in a big, open-ended feeder. You can scale up a bit, fishing for chub by this method, because once they get a taste they won't be too put off by the fact that you are using 3 lb line instead of 2 lb!

Offer the grub in multiples, after you have taken them out of the cake, or else fish a lump of cake with half a dozen grubs in. The latter stops on the hook better and would be a better bet if you were legering. If the going is really rough in winter, a single grub on a 18 or 20 has on numerous occasions provided a bite from a match winning chub.

To give you some idea of the pulling power of the grub, North Yorks and South Durham National man Dave Nicholson shattered the Trent four hour match record last season with 47 lb of chub on the wasp grub. If that doesn't convince you that you should really be out nesting in the summer, then nothing else will. When I tell you that he collected a pillowcase full of nests the day before the match from the very banks of the river, then you'll realize its potential.

16 Groundbait

The use of groundbait in today's match circuit plays a bigger part than ever. Groundbaiting, many years ago, used to be a case of 'if the fish come, fill it in' and whilst this may have worked to a certain extent, on today's hard-fished bream venues such a tactic would be fatal. Of all the rivers on the open match circuit, the Witham used to receive more attention than most. Until a few years ago it was normal practice to unload as much as ten balls for starters, as soon as the whistle went. The thinking behind this was, 'if there's any bream there, then a load of groundbait will stop them moving to the next man'. Well, times have changed and now, the principle is only to feed for bream when you are pretty certain that they aren't there! Groundbait, its texture, composition and the feed that goes into it, is now regarded as of utmost importance. I'm sure years ago the top anglers had plenty of tricks up their sleeves, but today the competition is so fierce that no thinking match angler can afford to let this be a weak link in his armoury.

Texture and composition

Ideally, groundbait should be made from bread, both white and brown crumbs. White crumb mixes harder and can be thrown a good deal further than brown, but dependant on distance, a satisfactory mixture of the two can usually be arrived at. The formulae should be based on how far the mix has to travel, how soft it can be and how much feed can be packed into it. On a bream venue or a still water it isn't good policy to have a bed of white groundbait on the bottom. This makes the fish edgy and they will be loth to move onto it to feed. Long distance groundbaiting is often required, however, and so a small amount (the least possible) of white must be mixed in to hold the ball together, and the texture should be gauged so that the ball breaks up as quietly as possible on impact. You will also have to take into account just how much feed you can possibly pack into the feed. The more the better, because it's the casters, worms and squatts that the bream are interested in, not the breadcrumbs.

When fishing deep, fast flowing rivers, such as the Wye, Severn, Ribble or Tyne, then the ratio of white to brown can be increased, not only to get the bait down within the confines of your swim, but to enable you to pack as much feed as necessary to keep the large shoals of fish consolidated.

On canals or slow moving rivers, such as the Great Ouse, Thames or Weaver, where roach and skimmers are often encountered, then the crumb itself can be riddled much finer and introduced much softer, to create less disturbance. The use of catapults in propelling groundbait has enabled the match angler to mix his groundbait much softer. The sudden flexing of the elbow, when throwing by hand, would break up the softer mix now normally employed. The advantage of the catapult is that the acceleration is smooth and, more important, the ball doesn't spin in the air if fired smoothly. Throwing it by hand, it is very difficult to stop the ball turning as it leaves the palm of the hand, and this is one of the major causes of groundbait disintegrating in mid-flight.

Soil can also be addeed to groundbait, to give a darker texture and to give extra 'body' for getting distance. Soil from molehills makes an excellent additive and on the Trent and Welland, to name but two venues, this is now a popular ploy.

When and how to use groundbait

When, is the big question. Groundbait has two purposes and if you don't need to use it for either of these, then you would be better off loose feeding in most circumstances. Its main object is to carry feed through the water in heavy flow, when loose feed wouldn't get down in the confines of your peg and to project your loose feed further than you could with a catapult. In both cases accuracy is of paramount importance, because your feed is packed so tightly that there is no room for error. Groundbait often works close in, on the upper Trent for example, and it ensures that you have a tight line of feed to fish down to.

Some waters take groundbait, others don't. Local knowledge is important, though it often pays to do something different from what local trends dictate. The Ladbrokes Super League in 1977 was a classic example, when Ivan Marks took his team to Evesham on the Warwickshire Avon. Against all the odds they used groundbait, anathema to the locals, and swept the board not once but twice. There can be no hard and fast rules, as you can see, but if in doubt start gently and play it by ear.

Mixing groundbait and throwing it causes people all sorts of problems, and really it shouldn't. It pays to buy your groundbait in bulk, for in that way you will be able to judge after a few outings how it is going to mix and perform for you, just how much water to add, and when it feels right for the particular job you want it to perform.

There is a time in every match angler's career when he has thrown a ball of groundbait and wished the ground would open up and swallow him, for the ball has broken up in mid-air and plastered half the river, from middle to far bank. There are two main causes. The first is the consistency of the groundbait. Either the mix is too wet, or there are just too many feeders inside and they have broken it up in mid-flight. Maggots and pinkies are the main culprits and generally aren't recommended as feeders for long distance work. The second cause for

The groundbait catapult has given a lot more anglers the chance to compete (© Jim Lauritz)

groundbait breaking up in mid-flight is because, when the ball was thrown the angler hadn't wetted his hands. It's surprising how many anglers don't realize that if your throwing hand still has groundbait on it (and so you aren't throwing from a smooth surface), then the ball will slightly stick to the palm of your hand as it leaves. This is quite enough to cause it to fracture and, as it spins through the air, more often than not it will break. The problem is easily solved. As soon as you have mixed the ball, lay it down for a second, rinse your hands, pick it up again, give it another quick moulding and you'll find that it flies as sweet and true as it ever has done. Get into the habit of doing it every time and you should never have to hang your head in shame again!

Catapulting groundbait has given a lot more anglers the chance to compete, anglers who previously couldn't throw for toffee. Catapults can cause problems as well, however, mostly for the same reasons as those encountered by hand throwers. Groundbait encrusted in the pouch, over-stretching the capabilities of the catapult, and an unsteady release can all make for difficulties. Let the catapult do the work, don't try and help it on its way.

Practice makes perfect, whether throwing or catapulting. Go and watch the top men throw groundbait, men like Ivan Marks and Jim Todd, and they make it look so effortless and easy that you'll wonder what all the fuss was about. It still pays to be able to throw, as opposed to catapult, because you can put in far larger quantities more quickly by hand and in Ireland, for example, this is a great advantage.

17 Clothing

Winter

There is at present such a bewildering selection of winter wear clothing on the market that match anglers could be forgiven for being confused and spoilt for choice. Some clothing is good, some not so good, but there is so much to choose from that no self-respecting angler should ever be uncomfortable, even in the harshest of conditions.

The two main criteria by which clothing should be judged are:

1. Will it keep me warm and dry?
2. Will it give me freedom of movement?

If the answers to those two questions are in the affirmative, then you are well on the way to solving your winter clothing problems.

The three parts of your body most vulnerable to cold are the head, hands and feet. It is no coincidence that these parts of the anatomy are at the extremities, and because you are liable to be sitting or standing all day, the circulation of blood is going to be weak, especially to the feet and hands. Keeping warm and dry is not solved by putting on mounds of clothing; this may work whilst you are walking to your peg, but once you sit down the surface circulation of warm air given off by the body is going to be restricted and you will soon get cold again.

The first priority is a good outer garment. The current trend is for a waterproof, one-piece suit and there is no doubt that these do a first rate job of beating the wind and wet. A one-piece suit with a hood is a wise investment. For the feet you have two alternatives. If you are going to be in the water up to your knees then waders are essential. Coupled with a pair or even two pairs of thick woollen socks, then you should be able to combat the cold. Wellingtons and socks made from synthetic fibres are a bad combination. Nylon and other synthetics do not let your skin breathe and so restrict the flow of warm air.

If you aren't going to be wading, then either a pair of knee or calf length boots would be ideal. Derry boots or similar are very popular and once again, worn in conjunction with a natural wool, they will keep your feet

More and more team and individual anglers are now taking much more care with their appearance. Ex-world champion Pierre Michiels of Belgium, seen here at Angling 76, *is a good example (© David Hall)*

warm and dry for many hours. Rubber, even though unavoidable with waders, in any other form isn't recommended, as it seems to have very low insulation properties and the heat seems to flow out as quickly as the cold gets in. Unprotected hands are another source of coldness and depression on the bankside. There are many brands of mittens for sale and unlike gloves, these will give you freedom to handle your tackle, tie hooks, put bait on, etc. If you can't wear mittens, and there are plenty of people who can't, then a quick smear of *Vaseline* over the back of your hands insulates the skin from the cold wind and offers a great deal of relief. It's well worth trying.

The head and neck should also receive priority when it comes to dressing to beat the cold. Assuming that you have a one-piece suit with a hood it also helps if you can wear a balaclava. A hood only loosely protects, whereas a woollen balaclava fits the contours of your neck and head and will keep you very warm indeed.

Underneath your one piece suit you will also need to dress sensibly. Jeans are all very well, but you would be better off with a thick pair of corduroys or similar. The top half of your body should really have the first layer of clothing in cotton, once again a natural material. Building up from that, then it would be practical to have a thin sweater and on top of that a thick sweater. If, as the day wears on, you become too warm, then you can always take your top sweater off.

There is also a trend towards wearing a one-piece under-vest. In very cold, bitter conditions this would be a valuable asset. They are lightweight and don't restrict your movement. They are, however, highly effective insulators and if the day turns out to be very warm, then there's a good chance you could roast alive. But, in the British climate, especially in winter, I think I would be prepared to take the chance.

Summer

Clothing for summer fishing has none of the problems associated with keeping warm and dry during the cold winter months. Of course you can still expect the odd rainy day, and the obvious answer to this is a lightweight jacket (with overtrousers, if necessary). It was often suggested that fish are wary of bright colours on the bankside, and to a certain extent this theory would appear to be sound. Bearing that in mind it would be advisable to opt for colours other than bright orange, yellow or white. Brown, green and dark blue are the obvious choices for lightweight jackets and as long as the material allows you freedom of movement then the choice is wide open. One item of summer clothing that is fast gaining popularity is the simple waistcoat, with plenty of side pockets. If it's a hot day then the sleeveless waistcoat allows the top half of your body to breathe (the circulation of air keeps you cool), as well as giving your arms complete freedom of movement for casting and striking.

Eyeshades are a necessity, both in summer and winter, for the glare of a rippled surface can play havoc with the keenest eyesight, in watching a float or a swingtip. It's a good idea to line the eyeshade with towelling, not only to protect the skin from abrasion but to act as a sweatband as well. More and more team and individual anglers are now taking far more care in their appearance on the bankside, and this in itself is an important step forward in establishing the sport of match fishing in the eyes of the public and media. Everyone will freely admit that a smart jacket, with the names of team and sponsors on the back, isn't going to catch you any more fish, but it does plenty of other things to establish match angling. A well turned out squad is more likely to attract sponsorship from enlightened tackle companies than is a team of ungroomed louts in jeans and T-shirts, however good anglers they may be. A smartly turned out squad of anglers is of far greater benefit to the sport in the long run. For many years match angling has had a cloth cap image, but look at lesser sports and the publicity and sponsorship they attract and the reason isn't hard to see. If you saw a cyclist in the Tour de France on television pedalling away, dressed in trousers, a flat hat and cycle clips, bearing the name of a sponsor on his back, then you wouldn't take it seriously. By the same token, it will be hard work to attract more money and interest to the sport if we all turn out week after week looking like refugees, dressed in shabby boiler suits, wellingtons and bush hats.

The choice is yours, gentlemen. If you see your match fishing as merely a bit of light relief at the weekend and you don't care if the sport attracts more coverage, then fair enough. If however you want some fresh blood pumping into the sport, then we have to achieve a certain degree of credibility and you'll never do that in cloth caps and boiler suits . . . however lucky they may be for you.

18 Match Fishing Tomorrow

Practice and skill will eventually be rewarded when the draw bag gives you half a chance (© Jim Lauritz)

It is hoped that the preceding chapters have thrown light on some aspects of match fishing for all matchmen. There can't be an angler born who can hope to know it all: reading through the various pieces, I have been very glad to add to my general angling knowledge, and I don't doubt the reader will be as well.

What is apparent is, that each region breeds its own style of angler, who adapts to his own particular waters and evolves a method to win. The formula can clearly be repeated on other rivers with just as much success. The Birmingham and Leicester lads, highly successful on their home waters, can go to rivers further afield and with quiet confidence adapt to strange waters and show the rest of the field a clean pair of heels, which tends to scotch the theory that they can only perform on certain waters.

Nothing could be further from the truth, as they have proved over and over again. Ron Lees, for example, made his name on the Severn, yet his meat fishing methods will work on any chub water. Stan Piecha's long range float tactics can be adapted to a multitude of waters and Mike Winney's swimfeeder piece can be adapted to any flowing water with a head of big fish.

Of course, slight alterations would have to be made, but that is the name of the game, in a word, versatility. The angler who can adapt and adapt quickly when he realizes that a change, however slight will make all the difference between catching enough to get in the frame and being an also ran, is the angler who makes the grade. What makes an angler versatile? The big question. Many will tell you that such anglers make changes and decisions in a match without really thinking about it, they are intuitive. For those who don't possess that gift, then it all comes down to having a good memory, remembering what happened in a similar circumstance, maybe seasons ago. An angler with a sharp memory has a valuable asset, one which if used and capitalized upon puts him head and shoulders above the angler who fishes by the book. Dedication is therefore all important if you really want to make the grade, and as only a very small percentage can be at the top, then hard work, practice and skill will be eventually rewarded when the draw bag gives you half a chance. No-one can catch fish that aren't there and it is possible to go a long time making the most diabolical draws. It happens to everyone. There's little you can do about it, except persevere, in the knowledge that the law of averages will favour you with a run at the draw and then you have no excuse.

The biggest boost our sport could now receive is for the England squad to win the world championship. Many times we have let ourselves believe that we were close and though our record over the past few years has generally been good, one can't help feeling that the squad we have has been let down. Leadership must be set by example and the general feeling is that until you pass over the reins to proven, capable hands, then the squad will never give of its best. The world championship may be a glorious day out for some of our more politically minded officials and supposed leaders, but the time has now come to hand over the team management to people who actually still go fishing and succeed, rather than to entrusting the team to organisers of people, who have had more than their fair crack of the whip. If England do win the championship and we have the men to do it, under the present management, it will be in spite of, not because of their presence. In fishing the world championship, the only thing at stake is the country's pride and the hopes of thousands of matchmen. It's time for a change, let's hope it's soon.

Index

Set by Cold Composition Ltd., Tonbridge,
and printed in Great Britain at the Anchor Press, Tiptree